Fawcett Premier Books by
Robert Goldston:

THE RUSSIAN REVOLUTION

THE CIVIL WAR IN SPAIN

THE LIFE AND DEATH OF NAZI GERMANY

THE RISE OF RED CHINA

THE GREAT DEPRESSION

COMMUNISM: A NARRATIVE HISTORY

Robert Goldston

THE LIFE AND DEATH OF
NAZI GERMANY

卐 卐 卐 卐 卐 卐 卐 卐 卐 卐

FAWCETT PREMIER • NEW YORK

A Fawcett Premier Book
Published by Ballantine Books

Copyright © 1967 by Robert Goldston

ACKNOWLEDGMENTS:
The author owes a debt of gratitude to the following publishers and authors for permission to quote from the following works: *Austrian Requiem* by Dr. Kurt von Schuschnigg, translated by Franz von Hildebrand, G. P. Putnam's Sons, copyright © 1946; *Hitler's Interpreter* by Paul Schmidt, Macmillan Company, copyright © 1951; *Nuremberg Diary* by Dr. G. M. Gilbert, Farrar, Straus & Giroux, Inc., copyright © 1947; *The Ciano Diaries, 1939–1943* edited by Hugh Gibson, Doubleday & Company, Inc., copyright © 1946, courtesy of Edda Ciano; *The Goebbels Diaries, 1942–43* edited by Louis P. Lochner, Doubleday & Company Inc., copyright © 1948; *The Speeches of Adolph Hitler* edited by Norman H. Baynes, Oxford University Press, copyright © 1942; *They Almost Killed Hitler* by Fabian von Schlabrendorff and Gero v. S. Gaevernitz, Macmillan Company, copyright © 1947, courtesy of Gero von S. Gaevernitz.

ISBN 0-449-30030-7

This edition published by arrangement with
The Bobbs-Merrill Company, Inc.

Manufactured in the United States of America

First Fawcett Premier Edition: January 1969
First Ballantine Books Edition: November 1983
Second printing: October 1985

Contents

THE LIFE AND DEATH OF
NAZI GERMANY

Prologue

A PROBLEM OF HISTORY

ON THE MORNING OF NOVEMBER 20, 1945, THE CEN-
tral courtroom in the fortress-prison at Nuremberg,
Germany, was filled to capacity—and absolutely still.
Sunlight, flickering through the high, Gothic-style windows of the old stone building, fell upon a scene of
tense drama unique in the history of the world. For in
this drab and drafty room an International Military Tri-
bunal appointed by the victors of World War II had
brought to trial the top leaders of a defeated nation, accused of crimes against the peace and against humanity.
There were some in the courtroom and beyond it who
doubted whether any court had the right to judge the
activities of a formerly sovereign nation; others dismissed the trial as nothing more than the vengeance of
the victors over the vanquished. But most people hoped
and prayed that from these proceedings new standards
of international law and morality might arise.

The crowd of spectators, both military and civilian;
the intent reporters representing newspapers from every
corner of the world; the United States Army military
police standing stiffly at "parade rest" near the doors;
the august judges—American, British, French, and

9

Russian—presiding at the bench; the defendants shift-
ing uneasily on their benches in the prisoners' dock: all
were listening in wondering silence as prosecution attor-
neys took turns reading the indictment against the accused:

"Count One: The Common Plan or Conspiracy . . .
The acquiring of totalitarian control in Germany . . .
Utilization of Nazi control for foreign aggression. . . .
Count Two: Crimes against Peace . . . Violation of in-
ternational treaties, agreements, and assurances. . . .
Count Three: War Crimes . . . Murder and ill-treat-
ment of civilian populations and prisoners of war . . .
Deportation for slave labor . . . Killing of hostages.
. . . Count Four: Crimes against Humanity . . . Mur-
der, extermination, enslavement . . . Persecution on
political and racial grounds . . ."

As the words of the indictment rang implacably
through the stillness of the courtroom, all eyes were
turned upon the defendants. There they were—the surviving members of the Nazi government of Germany:
Hermann Goering, chief of the German Air Force,
President of the German parliament, taker of drugs,
murderer of military hostages, international thief;
Joachim von Ribbentrop, Foreign Minister, plotter of
wars, breaker of treaties, betrayer of his word; *Ernst
Kaltenbrunner,* Chief of Secret Police, political murderer, assassin of untold thousands, common thug;
Hans Frank, Governor General of Poland, extermina-
tor of millions of men, women, and children; *Julius
Streicher,* Governor of Franconia, Jew-baiter, semiliter-
ate pornographer; and the others, twenty-three in all,
twenty-three men of low intelligence, cynical immoral-
ity, criminal backgrounds, and base tastes; the government of a modern, supposedly civilized nation.

The vilest members of the Nazi regime—*Heinrich
Himmler,* supreme boss of the dread SS, the man ultimately responsible for the murder of millions in con-

centration and extermination camps throughout Europe; *Paul Josef Goebbels,* propagandist extraordinary and liar par excellence, who had sickened and defiled the opinions of millions throughout Europe; and, of course, *Adolf Hitler,* the leader, the destroyer of nations, the would-be conqueror of the world, the insane architect of German triumph and disaster—these men chose suicide rather than face judgment.

And if the men who had ruled Germany were now either dead or prisoners, their works were still plainly visible beyond the walls of Nuremberg prison—in the devastated cities of Europe, in the smoking towns and hamlets of a continent, in the millions of orderly white crosses in a hundred military cemeteries, in the ruins of extermination camps where mountains of clothing, of children's toys, testified to the cremation of a race. And visible too in the mute anguish of the survivors and in the stunned faces of the victors were the frightening questions that clamored for an answer at Nuremberg.

How could these defendants—who should have long since been confined to prisons or asylums or the sewers from which they had sprung—have come to rule one of the most powerful nations in the world? Who or what was responsible for that basic crime against sanity? Who or what was responsible for the atrocious crimes committed in the name of that government? Who was on trial here, only the government of Germany or the entire German nation? Or did all peoples everywhere somehow bear responsibility for the terrible events recited in the indictment at Nuremberg?

So frightful was the impact of Nazi Germany upon the consciousness and conscience of mankind that even today, more than twenty years later, many people still cannot bring themselves to believe it all really happened, that it was all true. It is with a feeling of numb frustration that we still ask ourselves apparently unanswerable questions:

How could so literate a country, the country of such writers as Johann Wolfgang von Goethe, Heinrich Heine, Friedrich von Schiller, Thomas Mann, become the scene of book burning and thought control? How could so intellectually developed a nation, the nation of Martin Luther, Karl Marx, Immanuel Kant, Albert Einstein, launch itself upon so basically stupid an adventure as world conquest? How could so sensitive a people, the people of Johann Sebastian Bach, Ludwig van Beethoven, Johannes Brahms, Richard Strauss, participate in the organized and pitiless mass slaughter of millions of defenseless and innocent men, women, and children? Even on a strictly practical level, how could a country with so notable a military tradition, the country of Frederick the Great, Karl von Clausewitz, the Great General Staff, Count Helmuth von Moltke, Erich Ludendorff, stumble into the greatest military catastrophes of modern history?

Some of the permanent factors that have influenced German history can be deduced from geography. The land itself is a broad plain, bounded on the north by the North Sea and the Baltic Sea and rising through hilly regions to its majestic southern border of Austrian Alps and the mountains of Bohemia. Although it is traversed by three large rivers—the Rhine, the Elbe, and the Oder—the north German plain has no significant natural boundaries to either east or west. It has always been a broad highway of commerce—and of invasion—between Asia and Europe.

Most German borders have always been artificial—therefore impermanent—and this has perhaps helped to create a permanent sense of national insecurity. Furthermore, their position as the people of the middle —between the Slavic East and the Latin West—may also explain a certain dualism in the German national character. Since earliest times they have found themselves imitating the more highly developed culture of the West while carrying on constant war and conquest in the more backward East.

The word "German" (derived from the name of one of a number of tribes) was used by Tacitus and other Roman historians to denote all the barbarians living east of the Rhine, north of the Danube, and west of the Vistula. From the time of Julius Caesar these tribes were in a more or less permanent state of border warfare against the Roman Empire.

But while Germans infiltrated the decaying Roman Empire to the west, they themselves remained under constant pressure from even more barbaric tribes to the east. It was this pressure from Slavs, Huns, and other Asiatic peoples that resulted in the mass migrations of the Germanic tribes westward and culminated with the conquest of western Gaul (present-day France) by the Franks and the eruption of the Vandals and Goths into Spain and Italy, which helped bring the Roman Empire in the west to an end.

Charlemagne the Great, a Frankish king, succeeded in conquering and unifying the Franks, Saxons, Bavarians, and other Germanic tribes at the end of the eighth century A.D., and in the year 800, Charlemagne caused himself to be crowned emperor of what he was pleased to call the "Holy Roman Empire" and what later German historians referred to as the First Reich (a word best translated as "dominion over"). But Charlemagne's empire did not long survive his death. It was split into three parts by the Treaty of Verdun in 843, and later attempts to reunite it never achieved more than momentary or partial success. The office of emperor became an elective one (the Emperor being chosen by local dukes, bishops, and other notables), while the Holy Roman Empire itself soon came to represent only the less and less obedient principalities of Germany and northern Italy. Nevertheless, the glory of Charlemagne lived on in legend and song (the ancient warrior-king and his knights waiting eternally for the flourish of trumpets, the dawn of a new day of supreme power) to haunt German memories and inspire German ambition ever after.

By the fifteenth century the prestige of the Holy Roman Emperor had fallen to its lowest level. The title was considered to be an empty one and, almost as a gesture of contempt, the feudal lords of Germany conferred it upon a member of the Hapsburg family. But the Hapsburgs turned out to be surprisingly able politicians whose chief weapon—advantageous marriages —brought them within a century to very real power throughout Europe. Thus when the Hapsburg Charles V was elected Holy Roman Emperor in 1519, his family possessions, extending from the Netherlands to Spain and from Italy to Bohemia, hemmed in the German feudal lords on all sides. At last it seemed that the moment for a final struggle against feudalism and for the unification of Germany had arrived.

But two upheavals, one economic and the other spiritual, prevented this from occurring. First of all, the great German trading cities, Hamburg and Cologne, and the Hanseatic ports, entered a period of decline as English and Dutch merchants, taking advantage of new geographic discoveries, assumed the leadership in world trade. From having been a center of world commerce, Germany became an economic backwater.

The second upheaval commenced on October 31 in the year 1517, when an obscure Augustinian friar named Martin Luther nailed to the door of the castle church in the town of Wittenberg 95 theses for the reform of the Catholic Church.

Although he was promptly declared a heretic, Luther's words and example could not be suppressed. They were one of the sparks which ignited the great

Protestant Reformation that was now to sweep Europe.

Then, in June of 1524, aroused by Luther's teachings but rooted in centuries of misery and oppression, a peasant rebellion broke out which soon spread throughout south and west Germany. Luther himself, appalled by the ferocity and desperate savagery of the impoverished peasants, sided with the nobility and the feudal lords, urging them to suppress the uprising and punish the peasants severely.

But the impact of Lutheranism upon the German national character was far deeper than its immediate consequences. By his brilliant translation of the Latin Bible into everyday German, Luther did much to establish the national language. By his subservience to the local princes and his teaching that the state could do no wrong (to the individual conscience) he established a pattern for German behavior toward official authority which has endured to our own time.

The moment for German unification once lost in the sixteenth century was not to return for more than three hundred years. The Holy Roman Empire remained as an insubstantial and shadowy entity to haunt European history but not to affect it. Spasmodic efforts by succeeding Hapsburg emperors to unite the independent principalities of Germany led, in 1618, to the confused and calamitous Thirty Years' War in which France, Sweden, and Denmark intervened repeatedly to prevent German unification under Hapsburg rule. This war, which devastated Germany from end to end, laying waste great areas and depopulating entire districts, ended very much where it had begun —with Germany still divided into many petty states.

During all the centuries of conflict to unite the German states in the west, Germans in the east had carried on a campaign of endless conquest and extermination against their Slav and Polish neighbors. One result of the steady expansion eastward was the gradual creation of the state of Prussia—a sandy frontier region with a capital, Berlin, which was little more than a military camp. Lying east of the river Elbe, Prussia was the result of true colonial conquest. Its original Slav and Polish inhabitants had long been either exterminated or impressed into slavery by the military border lords who had conquered them. Chief among these lords and eventually the hereditary rulers of Prussia were the Hohenzollerns.

The development of Prussia into an important power was almost the decision of a single man—the Hohenzollern Frederick II, known to history as Frederick the Great. From the moment he ascended the throne of Prussia (in 1740) his policy was to be one of expansion and conquest. The seizure of Silesia from the Hapsburg Empress Maria Theresa of Austria in 1742 gave Prussia an industrial area, while Frederick's participation in the slicing up of Poland between Prussia, Austria, and Russia in 1772 made Prussia the largest and most powerful of the northern German states. But if Frederick the Great had raised Prussia to the ranks of the great powers, equipped her with an army second to none in Europe and made her a viable national state, he had done nothing to use that power for the unification of the German states. The Prussian drive for conquest in Germany itself was to be caused by revolutionary events beyond the frontiers of Germany.

The spark came with the French Revolution of 1789—a revolution which was to change the structure of German life. For as the French Napoleonic armies spilled over the Rhine they brought with them not only military supremacy but the seeds of revolutionary thought. Wherever French arms were supreme, there the French Revolutionary ideals were implanted. And Napoleon himself, more interested in power than in ideals, in 1806 brought to an end that ancient political fiction which was neither holy, Roman, nor an empire. In its place Napoleon created the Confederation of the Rhine, a loose organization of most of the thirty German "independent" states under French control.

To the Prussians their defeat at Napoleon's hands brought a sudden and sharp awakening; if Prussia was to survive at all, it would have to depend on the active support of all its people. This was to be accomplished basically by abolishing serfdom, introducing universal military service, opening the officer corps to men of ability from all classes, and instituting a system of popular education from primary school to university level. And so well did the reorganizers of the Prussian Army such as Gerhard von Scharnhorst and August Neithardt von Gneisenau do their work that the new and completely reorganized Prussian Army was able to make a large contribution in the Allied campaigns of 1813, which brought Napoleon's empire to its end.

In the spring of 1815 the victorious Allies, meeting in the Congress of Vienna, attempted to give Germany a new political organization. But the events of the Napoleonic era could not be simply repealed. Thus the Napoleonic reorganization of Germany was not seriously altered. The "Confederation of the Rhine" became the "German Confederation," and this new confederation was given a federal parliament which had almost no powers over its member states.

A more important change was the granting to Prussia of the northern half of the Kingdom of Saxony and the lower half of the Kingdom of Westphalia. For with these new territories Prussian power was firmly established on the Rhine, and Prussia became in effect the defender of the German states against any renewal of French aggression.

By 1848 the heavy stagnation of the Vienna settlement had become completely undermined—not by rev-

olutionary fervor, but by the economic crisis of the
1840's, which brought widespread depression to German peasants and mass unemployment to the city populations. Sparked by the uprising of the workers in
Paris in that year, similar street riots, disorders, and
outright rebellions broke out in Vienna, Berlin, and the
cities of the German Confederation.

Meeting in Frankfurt in the spring of 1848, delegates from all over Germany constituted themselves
into a pre-parliament which became known as the
Frankfurt Assembly. Immediately they proposed far-
reaching reforms in German life. Universal suffrage
was to be instituted and an all-German federal parliament elected which would truly rule the country. With
the Prussian and Austrian monarchies momentarily
helpless before the rebellions in their own territories,
and with the petty princes of the Confederation cowed
by the rise of republican sentiment all about them, it
appeared that a new and vital opportunity to establish
a liberal German state had arrived. But the appearance
was not the reality.

Just as the existence of the Frankfurt Assembly depended upon the temporary eclipse of Prussian and
Austrian military power, so its end was brought about
by a resurgence of that power. Typically, the crux of
the matter was not internal reform but external aggression. For the victory of German liberalism in 1848 had
encouraged the subject peoples of Prussia and Austria
—the Poles, Czechs, and Hungarians—to undertake
their own revolutions. It was in the suppression of these
uprisings that the Austrian and Prussian monarchies
regained power in their own dominions.

In April of 1849, Prussian troops put an end to the
debates of the Frankfurt Assembly by the simple expedient of chasing them out of Frankfurt. The year of
German liberalism thus ended in complete and utter
defeat. The old repressions, the old stagnation, the

rights of the princes and the power of Austria and Prussia, the disfranchisement of the masses, and the suppression of liberal thought came back with a vengeance.

But if the cause of liberalism was defeated in Germany, the cause of nationalism was not. During the next few years the steady growth of education, industrialization, and the improvement in communications wrought by the emerging railroad era were slowly but surely binding Germany into a whole. And in Prussia a new and more resolute monarch, William, had come to the throne. His prime minister was one of the ablest politicians in European history—Otto von Bismarck.

Having declared that "The great questions of the day will not be settled by resolutions and majority votes—that was the mistake of the men of 1848 and 1849—but by blood and iron," Bismarck addressed himself to a solution of the immediate problems of Prussia: the maintenance of Junker supremacy in an industrial society and the suppression of liberal sentiment throughout the German states.

Bismarck recognized that the answer to both these problems was nothing less than a conquest of Germany by Prussia. Only such a conquest could finally eliminate Austria from German affairs, and enable the Prussian ruling class effectively to stamp out the constant ferment of liberalism in the German states. Beyond that, Bismarck understood clearly that the burgeoning industrialization of Germany demanded the rationality of a unified German nation—and he was determined that the Hohenzollern dynasty should control that unification.

Within less than a decade Bismarck had maneuvered first Denmark, then Austria, and finally France into wars with Prussia. First the small Danish Army, then the clumsy Hapsburg forces, and ultimately the large but poorly led and equipped divisions of the corrupt French Emperor Napoleon III fell victim to the highly efficient Prussian Army led by a brilliant General Staff and the military genius of Count Helmuth von Moltke. During this process the small German states were reduced to absolute dependence upon Prussia while German political emotions were given a new and exciting outlet in the glory of the Hohenzollern victories. On the 18th of January in 1871, on the bones of a defeated and prostrate France, the German Empire was proclaimed with William of Prussia crowned Emperor William I of Germany in the Hall of Mirrors at Versailles. Thus in the space of ten years Bismarck succeeded in accomplishing what the preceding centuries had failed to produce: a unified Germany, the Second Reich.

This new Germany incorporated in itself all the contradictions, the compromises, and the impulses of its heritage. Thus, although a national Reichstag (parliament) based on universal suffrage was called into existence in Berlin, its powers were strictly limited to approving or disapproving new laws (it could not originate new laws by itself) and voting the federal budget. And although the states were now subordinated to the empire, their rulers retained their local titles, while their separate interests were represented in Berlin by a Bundesrat (federal senate). The imperial government was composed of a cabinet with a chancellor (prime minister) who were responsible only to the Emperor, not to the Reichstag.

The basic aims of Bismarck's Germany were to preserve the privileges of the Prussian ruling class, the Prussian Army, and the Emperor. To keep the industrial workers relatively quiet Bismarck (between 1883 and 1889) introduced a widespread system of social security in the form of workers' accident, sickness, and old-age benefits. This system, along with legal repression of the Social Democratic party, the Marxist-oriented workers' movement, succeeded in stifling radical opposition temporarily. The industrial capitalists and grain-producing landlords were offered first, high protective tariffs and favorable taxes and, later, colonies for exploitation. The General Staff was assured of an ever-expanding army. And, although Bismarck's policy was one of peace, whenever discontent at home threatened his program, he did not fail to use the old rallying cry "Fatherland in Danger!" to stifle domestic opposition. France, Russia, England, each at one time or another was used as a bogey to frighten the German people into accepting a system which kept the Prussian ruling classes and the Emperor firmly in control of Germany. These were the balances of Bismarck's Germany, and his time as Chancellor was spent in one long juggling act.

In 1888 a new emperor came to the German throne. He was William II and he was destined to be the last emperor. A relatively young man (he was thirty at the time of his coronation), William II was aggressive, unstable, and utterly without political competence. But in dismissing Bismarck as Chancellor in 1890, the new emperor was simply expressing the logic of Bismarck's life's work. He *believed* Germany to be surrounded by evil-intentioned enemies, *believed* that the working class could be satisfied by continual economic bribes, *believed* that the industrial capitalists needed colonial expansion for markets and a powerful navy to protect those colonies, *believed* that as the God-anointed ruler of the German Empire his strength was unassailable.

The magic-shows with which Bismarck had disguised the basic contradictions of German life had become the reality of that life. And German fears, ambitions, and illusions ticked like a time bomb in the heart of Europe.

One

THE MIND OF A FANATIC

ADOLF HITLER, THE MAN WHO WAS ONE DAY TO IN-herit the power of Bismarck and of the emperor, was not born in Germany. He was born (at six thirty on the evening of April 20, 1889) in the little Austrian village of Braunau am Inn—just across the border from German Bavaria. Adolf's father, Alois Hitler, and his mother, Klara Poelzl, were second cousins; Adolf was their third son. Alois Hitler (who for the first forty years of his life had gone by his mother's name, Schicklgruber) was a minor Austrian customs official of unsettled habits and uncertain emotions. Klara Poelzl was his third wife and had been his housekeeper during the last years of Alois' second marriage.

In 1895, when Adolf Hiter was six years old, Alois retired from government service (he was fifty-eight) and for the next four or five years moved restlessly about from one village to another near the Austrian city of Linz. Adolf went to the village school at Fischlham, spent two years at the Benedictine Monastery at Lambach, and by the time he was fifteen had attended five different schools and lived in seven different towns. When he was eleven years old, he was sent to the high school in Linz, there to study to become a civil servant like his father. But the young Hitler had no desire to follow in his father's footsteps. As he wrote many years later in *Mein Kampf*:

I did not want to become a civil servant, no, and again, no. All attempts on my father's part to inspire me with love or pleasure in this profession by stories from his own life accomplished the exact opposite. . . . [I] grew sick to my stomach at the thought of sitting in an office . . . compelled to force the content of my whole life into paper forms. . . .

One day it became clear to me that I would become a painter, an artist. My father was struck speechless.

"Painter? Artist?"

He doubted my sanity, or perhaps he thought he heard wrong or misunderstood me. But when he was clear on the subject . . . he opposed it with all the determination of his nature.

"Artist! No! Never as long as I live!"

My father would never depart from his "Never!" And I intensified my "Nevertheless!"

Hitler later claimed that this quarrel with his father was the cause of his failure in high school. Although his grade school marks had been high, his work fell off so badly in high school that he eventually dropped out before graduating. Reminiscing in later years, Hitler was to claim:

"Our teachers were absolute tyrants. They had no sympathy with youth; their one object was to stuff our brains and turn us into erudite apes like themselves. If any pupil showed the slightest trace of originality they persecuted him relentlessly, and the only pupils whom I ever got to know have all been failures in afterlife."

On the other hand, his teachers had few illusions

about their pupil. They recalled him as being gifted but lazy, argumentative and bad-tempered.

In 1903 Alois Hitler died suddenly of a lung hemorrhage, leaving his widow, Klara (who was then forty-two), a very small pension on which to raise their two surviving children, Adolf and his sister Paula. And despite his mother's efforts to have him continue his education for the civil service, young Adolf dropped out of high school. Nor, in spite of the hardships his mother endured to stretch her meager income, did he think of getting a job. The idea of going to work to earn money was evidently repulsive to him then, and was to remain so for the rest of his life. Instead he spent the next three years roaming the pleasant Danubian countryside, dreaming away the days and reading away the nights. He went to the opera in Linz to hear the blood-tingling works of Wagner, wrote bad poetry (which he never sent) to a girl named Stephanie, and became interested in politics. By the time he was sixteen, he had already developed a violent hatred for the Hapsburg Monarchy of his native Austria-Hungary and a contempt for all the non-German elements of its population. He had already become obsessed with the glories of all things German.

But these halcyon years were brought to an end by two events which shocked Hitler into his first encounters with reality. The first was his rejection by the Vienna Academy of Fine Arts. Confident of his ability, he had applied for admittance in 1907, only to be told that he showed no promise at all as an artist and had best try for the School of Architecture. But here Hitler's lack of a high school diploma might prevent his entry. The second shock came with his mother's death at the end of 1907. To the nineteen-year-old Hitler ". . . it was a dreadful shock . . . I had honored my father, but my mother I had loved." And, perhaps worst of all, Hitler could no longer count on support from the family—he would be forced to earn a living. Although he had no trade—"With a suitcase full of clothes and underwear in my hand and an indomitable will in my heart, I set out for Vienna."

Hitler's years in Vienna, from 1909 to 1913, were to be filled with poverty, aimlessness, and despair. Earning a meager living shoveling snow or beating rugs or carrying suitcases at the railroad station, Hitler lived in flophouses and ate at charity kitchens. Nor was this the fault of the city. For Vienna, in the years just preceding the First World War, was not only charming—it was also prosperous. Penniless young men from the countryside could, with perseverance, earn a decent living—and trade unions were being established to secure workers' rights. Hitler's poverty was largely a matter of his own choice. For example, he never applied for entry to the School of Architecture, using his lack of a high school diploma as an excuse. Yet the school accepted students without high school diplomas if they showed sufficient promise. But Hitler preferred to avoid work as much as he could, supplementing his income from time to time by selling stilted and awkward drawings (usually copied from older works) which he sold to furniture dealers. The only activity which really attracted him was reading—and to that he devoted stupendous energy.

Already a teetotaler, a nonsmoker, and a vegetarian (as well as being afflicted with an incurable shyness toward women), Hitler expended himself in a voracious program of devouring books, mostly those dealing with German history or German mythology. He haunted the corridors of the Vienna libraries and, without the framework of an academic schooling, began to build a haphazard view of the world which he later recalled with the pride of the self-educated man: "In this period there took shape within me a world picture and a philosophy which became the granite foundation of all my acts. In addition to what I then created, I have had to learn little; and I have had to alter nothing."

What was this reading which so influenced the future dictator of Germany? It was undoubtedly mostly simplified commentary. Hitler never displayed the mental discipline that would have enabled him to make a thorough study of German philosophy in the original. But in the simplified forms with which he was able to cope, Hitler's later writings, speeches, and thought were largely based on ideas to be found in the nineteenth-century German philosophers Fichte, Hegel, Treitschke, and Nietzsche, and in the works of an Englishman, Houston Stewart Chamberlain.

Johann Gottlieb Fichte, in his "Addresses to the German Nation," denounced the Latin races and the Jews as "decadent" and the source of human misery. Fichte assured the Germans that they were in fact a master race. The German language was the purest, the German mythology the noblest, the German character the strongest in the world. One day, Fichte preached, Germans would find their true place in the sun as world dominators led by a small "elite" group of men who would have no need for common human moral restraints.

Georg Hegel, a philosopher of tremendous influence and brilliant mind (it was from Hegel's teachings that Marxism was later to emerge), taught that the national state was the highest form of human expression on earth. Compared to the state, the individual human being was of no importance whatsoever. His duty was to lose his identity in that of the state, thereby justifying his existence if not wholly excusing it. There is no place in Hegel's cosmos for human happiness—all that is a delusion. The force that moves not only history but human evolution forward is war. The German state has a special mission to perform—to regenerate the world through war—and it will be led in this mission by a special breed of "Heroes."

Heinrich von Treitschke believed that the unimportant individuals subject to the state should consider themselves slaves. It was unimportant what they thought, Treitschke held, so long as they obeyed. War was not only desirable, it was a logical necessity and the highest moral good. It purified and advanced the human race. Thus the glory of Prussian arms should be the greatest pride of the German nation.

Friedrich Wilhelm Nietzsche contributed to the Nazi mode of thought through his conception of the superman. This was to be the product of the evolution of an elite race (the Germans, of course) who would not fail to produce a man of profound intellect, great physical strength, tremendous moral courage, et cetera. And this superman and his elite followers would have no use for the laws and customs and moralities of ordinary mortals, for they would be lords of the earth.

But perhaps the most immediately important influence on Hitler's thought was to be found in the work of Chamberlain, who married a German girl, settled in Germany, and eventually renounced his British citizenship to become a German. Chamberlain's prime obsessions were the German nation and its destiny, the myth of race, and the perfidy of the Jews. Chamberlain believed that all of human history could be understood and explained on a racial basis. And of course the Aryan German race was the noblest in the world, destined to rule all humanity. As for the Jews, they were corrupt, a "negative" race. And what of Christ, whose nobility of spirit Chamberlain hated? Of course he could not have been a Jew. In fact he was an Aryan! Finally, Chamberlain argued, the German nation had the right and the duty to conquer the world because of its racial supremacy. Chamberlain's fame spread far and wide beyond the Rhine, and he became an intimate of Emperor William II, an adviser of the German government, and after Germany's defeat in World War I, a prophet of the rise of Adolf Hitler. Chamberlain, who died in 1927, met Hitler briefly in 1924 and immediately saw in him the God-appointed leader of the German people to their rightful place in the sun.

If the young Hitler spent much of his time in the Vienna libraries gleaning at second hand this preposterous hodgepodge of philosophy and speculation, he also had much to learn from the practical, day-to-day life of the great city which was the capital of the Hapsburg Empire. He read the newspapers avidly, devoured political pamphlets by the thousand, and even practiced his oratory on his fellow flophouse inmates. The Vienna of 1909-1913 was a city which reflected the decay of the Hapsburg Monarchy. Within the Austro-Hungarian Empire its subject peoples—the Czechs, the Hungarians, the Slavs, the Italians—were pressing for more and more independence from the German-Austrian government. And along with this nationalistic unrest there was also widespread social revolt. The suppressed working classes of the Hapsburg dominions were demanding the right to organize trade unions, the right to vote, the right to strike. They had organized themselves into a Social Democratic party theoretically based on the Communist teachings of Karl Marx and, by the time Hitler came to Vienna, were disputing parliamentary power with the middle-class Christian Socialists and the conservative Pan-German Nationalists. Hitler studied the methods of these three political parties carefully and reached certain conclusions.

First of all, much as he hated the Social Democrats for their internationalism and democratic ideals, he was forced to recognize that they knew how to organize a mass following for their program—they had mastered the art of propaganda. The Pan-German Nationalists, on the other hand, although their program of

suppression of other races, anti-Semitism, and antidem-
ocratic militarism appealed to Hitler, had, he decided,
made two grievous mistakes. They had failed to offer
any sort of economic or social bribe which would have
gained them the support of the militant working classes
and they had made an enemy of the Catholic Church,
thereby robbing themselves of important institutional
support. Besides that, they had failed to win the support of the Army—a cardinal error. As for the Christian Democrats, the party of the lower middle classes,
they certainly understood how to propagandize among
the masses, how to whip up enthusiasm by harping on
such issues as the "Jewish problem," and how to make
arrangements with such powers in the state as the
Army, the government, and the Church. But, although
their ideas were forceful, they failed to carry them out
to their logical conclusion. Thus, although they denounced the Jews, the Christian Democrats took no
real action against them, preferring to use anti-Semitism as a political weapon rather than as an objective
goal. And this, to Hitler, was a shameful betrayal of
principle.

It was from his close study of the tactics and programs of these political movements that Hitler's ideas
on the practicalities of power first developed. Later he
was to write of the Social Democrats:

I understood the infamous spiritual terror which this
movement exerts, particularly on the middle class, which
is neither mentally nor morally equal to such attacks; at a
given sign it unleashes a veritable barrage of lies and slan-
ders against whatever adversary seems most dangerous,
until the nerves of the attacked person break down. . . .
This is a tactic based on precise calculation of all human
weaknesses, and its results will lead to success with almost
mathematical certainty. . . . I achieved an equal under-

standing of the importance of physical terror toward the individual and the masses.

But this analysis had nothing to do with the tactics of the Social Democrats, who neither then nor later resorted to such means. It was instead a very accurate description of the political tactics of Hitler's own Nazi party. The fact that he ascribed it to the Social Democrats of his Vienna years can only be explained as due to his own prejudices, prejudices so strong that they caused him to project his own instincts onto his opponents.

According to Hitler, it was also during those years in Vienna that he came to hate the Jews. He described it as a spiritual revolution within himself and ascribed it to dedicated research as well as instinctual repulsion to individual Jews he observed on the street. But boyhood friends insisted that Hitler was an anti-Semite long before he came to Vienna. In any event, it was during those years that Hitler's hatred of the Jews developed into an all-consuming passion. That it represented a streak of insanity in him there can be little doubt. In the end this insane hatred was to lead to the greatest crimes in human history.

But if in Vienna Hitler developed his ideas of German racial superiority, the glory of war, the infamy of the Jews, the myth of the superman, the ruthless political tactics of gangsterism, the question may still be asked: Why did the mind of *this* young man in particular seek out and assimilate such poisonous thoughts?

Was his mind simply an extention of the brutishly ignorant peasant background from which he emerged? Had his personality been irretrievably damaged in conflict with his authoritarian father, smothered in the overprotection of his doting mother? Did his refusal to work, to study at school, to make a place for himself in the world, indicate a deep-seated and burning rage that the world had not recognized him simply by his presence? These questions fall under the discipline of psychological investigation and will probably never be completely answered. We can be certain only that a highly neurotic and unbalanced young man of vast ignorance and capable of hysterical hatreds found in Vienna a pattern of faith which suited him almost exactly. And by 1913, filled with loathing at the crumbling Hapsburg Monarchy, Hitler left Vienna to live in what he considered to be his logical and spiritual homeland—Germany.

Hitler was twenty-four when he left Vienna, and to all intents and purposes his years there had been wasted. He had not even tried to become an architect; his painting had never risen above the level of furniture decorating. He was a failure, without friends, family, or future. His only asset was a burning and fierce confidence (nonetheless real for being irrational) in his destiny. Acquaintances of his Vienna period recall the straggling black hair down over his collar, the pallor of his complexion, his thin, unwashed, and unkempt appearance, but they also recall the strange intensity in his eyes—the eyes of a fanatic.

Later it was said that Hitler left Vienna to escape Austrian military service. This was true. It was not due to cowardice but to a refusal to serve in an army which included Czechs, Slavs, and Jews. He wrote: "The longer I lived in [Vienna] the more my hatred grew for the foreign mixture of peoples which had begun to corrode this old site of German culture. . . . For all these reasons a longing rose stronger and stronger in me to go at last whither my childhood secret desires and secret loves had drawn me."

But Hitler's arrival in Munich did not bring any immediate change in his fortunes. There he found himself as lonely and poor as he had been in Vienna. It was not until one year after he arrived in the city that opportunity knocked, and only a mind as twisted as his would have considered it opportunity. For in the summer of 1914 Germany plunged into the First World War—and that dreadful holocaust which brought death and suffering to untold millions was, for the poverty-stricken outcast from Vienna, a heaven-sent chance to shed his past and lose himself in the glorious adventure of his adopted country. On August 3, 1914, Hitler petitioned King Ludwig III of Bavaria (one of the surviving princes of the German Empire) for permission to volunteer in a Bavarian regiment—and permission was granted.

"To me," he later observed, "those hours came as a deliverance from the distress that had weighed upon me during the days of my youth. I am not ashamed to say that, carried away by the enthusiasm of the moment, I sank down on my knees and thanked heaven out of the fullness of my heart for granting me the good fortune to be permitted to live in such a time. . . . . For me, as for every German, there now began the most memorable period of my life. Compared to the events of this gigantic struggle all the past fell away into oblivion."

So Adolf Hitler came to Germany, and arrived just in time to throw himself enthusiastically into the great war. His destiny was, from this time on, to be inseparably linked with that of his adopted Fatherland.

Two

WAR, DICTATORSHIP, AND THE WEIMAR REPUBLIC

PRINCE OTTO VON BISMARCK HAD ONCE PREDICTED THAT "some damned foolish thing in the Balkans" would start the next war. The foolish thing occurred when, on June 28, 1914, Serbian nationalists assassinated the Archduke Francis Ferdinand, heir to the Austro-Hungarian throne, in the little Balkan town of Sarajevo. The old Hapsburg Emperor Francis Joseph, embittered and humiliated and under the advice of Foreign Minister Count Berchtold, as ambitious as he was woolly-minded, determined to exact a heavy vengeance for this crime. On July 23 an Austrian ultimatum was delivered to Serbia, and even though the Serbs agreed to comply with most of its atrocious demands, the Austro-Hungarian Empire rejected the Serb answer and declared war on the tiny Balkan nation on July 28. The Austrians felt free to act in this manner largely because they had extracted a promise of support from Emperor William II of Germany. But even without that promise Germany would have gone to war to support her only ally in the event of a major conflagration.

The rest of the drama proceeded with the awful

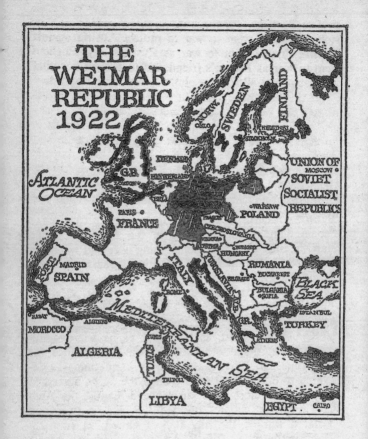

inevitability of a Greek tragedy. Russia went to war to protect Serbia, a Slav country, from Austrian aggression; Germany went to war to protect Austria against Russia; France went to war as Russia's ally; England went to war as France's friend and to protect her vital interests—and all Europe plunged into the holocaust.

So the enormous German armies, under the direction of the General Staff, moving according to a precise plan and with the efficiency of a machine, swept through Belgium and northern France. In the event, the German plan of conquest turned out to be beyond German capability. The swift victory planned by the General Staff eluded them, and in a series of desperate battles the French and British managed to stabilize the western front. In spite of tremendous victories in the east against the Czar's ill-equipped and demoralized armies, for Germany the war became one of grim survival in the face of an ever-tightening ring of enemies. By 1916 economic and military conditions in Germany had deteriorated to the point where neither the government nor the Emperor (whose grandiloquent title of Supreme War Lord rang ever more hollowly) could or would assume responsibility for German destinies, and that responsibility devolved naturally onto the General Staff.

The German General Staff, which traced its history back to the time of Frederick the Great, had over the centuries grown into an almost completely independent force within the structure of first the Prussian and later the German nation. As the supreme command of the Army, which was the basis of Prussia's existence and the dominant force in holding together the German Empire, the General Staff was responsible only to the Emperor, who in turn was expected to protect it against political assault within Germany. It was composed overwhelmingly of Junker aristocrats, trained in the soldierly virtues of courage, simple living, obedi-

ence, and ignorance in all that did not pertain to warfare. Its aims, which never varied, were, in descending
order of importance: to preserve the German Army; to
preserve the General Staff itself; to preserve the Hohenzollern Monarchy; to preserve Junker rule in Germany; to preserve Germany itself. And by 1916, with
the military war now inescapably bound up in an economic war of blockade and production, with the Emperor a mere spectator of events, with the German political parties unwilling and unable to direct German
life, the General Staff found itself in complete and supreme command of every aspect of Germany's beleaguered existence.

The dictatorship of the General Staff after 1916 was
embodied in the persons of Field Marshal Paul von
Hindenburg and General Erich Ludendorff. Von Hindenburg, a bluff old soldier whose first experience of
war had been against France in 1870, was little more
than a figurehead for the ruthless domination of Ludendorff, a much younger General Staff officer who
had won prominence by his capture of the Belgian fortress complex at Liège early in the war. Soon after that
Hindenburg and Ludendorff had planned the overwhelming German victories against the Russians at
Tannenberg and the Masurian Lakes. In the gray-
haired, fat old Field Marshal the German people saw a
reassuring and solid example of German power and
eventual German victory, while in Ludendorff they
thought they had found the keen intelligence and ruthless will that would ensure that victory.

The German people were very nearly right. Ludendorff, who, through the General Staff controlled almost
every aspect of German production, German planning,
and German manpower, was fanatically committed to
total war and total victory. His efforts during 1916,
1917, and the early months of 1918 brought complete
defeat to Russia and near-disaster to the Western Al-

lies. But with the entrance of the United States into the war in 1917 and the continuing ferocious resistance of British and French armies, accompanied by the strangulation of the British blockade, German defeat was not only unavoidable, it was at last apparent to the German General Staff.

On the home front, with starvation a daily possibility and the German economy in ruins, those German Socialists who had refused to support the war had formed a Communist party, known as the Spartacist League, under the dedicated leadership of Karl Liebknecht and Rosa Luxemburg. They, with certain other independent Socialists, were now demanding not only an end to the war but also a democratic socialist republic in Germany. And among the war-weary people of Germany and the growing thousands of disillusioned veterans they found greater and greater support. A mutiny broke out in the German fleet at Kiel in October of 1918; field divisions on the western front were refusing to fight any longer; antiwar strikes and demonstrations had erupted in most German cities. And, although Ludendorff and the General Staff were able to suppress the Kiel mutiny and probably could have controlled the rising tide of rebellion on the home front, continuing military disaster, including the collapse of Austria-Hungary and Bulgaria and a tremendous offensive by French, British, and American armies in the west made defeat certain.

The General Staff, which had always placed the Army, itself, and the Emperor before every other consideration, was now faced with a harsh choice. The Allies could not make peace with the Emperor, nor would they talk terms with Ludendorff, the military dictator. Yet the German Army needed peace desperately. It had been decisively defeated in the field, and by November of 1918 no General Staff officer could be found to deny that fact. It was at the insistence of the

Army and the General Staff that armistice negotiations were opened with the Allies; it was at their insistence that Allied terms were accepted. It is important to remember this fact, which was later denied by military leaders and gave rise to the legend that Germany's defeat had been due to subversion at home. Ludendorff was allowed to resign from command on October 26, 1918. Two weeks later, on November 9, Hindenburg (although he left the painful act to the new Chief of the General Staff, General Wilhelm Groener) informed the Emperor that he could no longer count on the loyalty of the German Army. William II thereupon abdicated and fled to Holland, and Bismarck's German Empire—the Second Reich—came to its disastrous and inglorious end.

The news of this calamity was brought to Corporal Adolf Hitler while he was recuperating from temporary blindness (suffered during a British gas attack) in the military hospital at Pasewalk, northeast of Berlin. A minister informed the wounded soldiers that the Emperor had abdicated, a German republic had been proclaimed in Berlin, and Germany had been defeated. The news came as a stunning blow to Hitler.

"I could stand it no longer," he later recalled. "Everything went black before my eyes; I tottered and groped my way back to the ward, threw myself on my bunk, and dug my burning head into my blankets and pillows . . . it had all been in vain."

During the four years and three months of the war, Hitler had been a brave soldier. Arriving at the front at the end of October 1914 as a dispatch runner with his Bavarian regiment, he had gone through the terrible first Battle of Ypres, where the British had halted the German offensive toward the Channel. Later he was wounded in the leg during the Battle of the Somme in October 1916. In March of 1917, promoted to corporal, he had fought at Arras. And on October

13, 1918, he had fallen before a British gas attack during the last Battle of Ypres. He was temporarily blinded and invalided to the hospital at Pasewalk. He won two decorations during the war: the Iron Cross, Second Class, in December 1914, and the Iron Cross, First Class, in August 1918, an award rarely bestowed on a common soldier at that time and one which unquestionably reflected personal bravery.

Like millions of other Germans, Hitler could not then or later bring himself to believe that the German Army had been defeated in the field. It must have been undermined at home—by the Democrats, the Socialists, the Jews, by any scapegoat that could be found to take the blame for Germany's unbelievable defeat. And events in Germany proceeded with a chaotic illogic which seemed to lend credibility to that lie.

On the afternoon of November 9, 1918, with the field armies streaming back to the Rhine in defeat; with disbanded regiments and swarms of deserters straggling across the countryside and already forming themselves into freebooting small armies for hire—the notorious Frei-korps; with soviet-style councils of workers and soldiers taking power in the provincial cities throughout Germany, some Social Democratic deputies to the Reichstag met in the cavernous halls of that great building on the Koenigsplatz in Berlin.

The Emperor had abdicated and fled; his last Chancellor, Prince Max of Baden, had resigned that very morning. A few blocks away from the Reichstag, in the former Imperial Palace, the Spartacists were preparing to declare Germany a Socialist Soviet Republic. The Social Democrats knew they had to act at once, but what to do? Outside the Reichstag, on the Koenigsplatz, a huge and sullen crowd awaited their decision.

The Social Democrats were under the leadership of Philipp Scheidemann and Friedrich Ebert, men to whom the entire idea of revolution was hateful. Ebert, for example, was still pondering—on that afternoon of November 9—whether it would not be possible to preserve the Hohenzollern Monarchy, perhaps with one of the Emperor's sons on the throne. But while he and his fellow deputies argued and worried, Philipp Scheidemann, on the spur of the moment, simply leaned his head out one of the Reichstag windows and proclaimed the establishment of a German Republic to the massed crowds below. Ebert was furious, the deputies bewildered, the crowd overjoyed, and thus Germany became a republic.

On the evening of November 9, as Ebert nervously pondered the future alone in the office of the Reich's Chancellor, the secret, direct telephone which connected that office with General Staff headquarters rang. Calling was General Wilhelm Groener, who only a few hours earlier had insisted on the Emperor's abdication. General Groener wanted to know if he could make a deal with Ebert. If Ebert and his Social Democratic followers were prepared to move decisively against the Spartacists, thereby saving Germany (and especially the General Staff) from a Bolshevik revolution, and if Ebert would maintain the Army and the General Staff in all its privileges, then Groener was prepared to guarantee General Staff and Army support for the newly declared German Republic. Ebert accepted the terms in relief—and thereby betrayed the Republic into the power of its enemies only a few hours after it had been proclaimed. For, although the General Staff needed the respectable "front" of a republican government in Berlin behind which to destroy the workers' revolution, deal with the Allies, and eventually rebuild German military power, under no circumstances could it be imagined that the German Officers' Corps would loyally serve a democratic society.

The new coalition of power was soon successful. On January 10, 1919, regular Army units, supported by groups of savage Free Corps troops, entered Berlin. With their usual ferocity they rounded up the Spartacists. Scores of workers were killed during the next seven days (which came to be known as "bloody week" in Berlin) while Karl Liebknecht and Rosa Luxemburg were captured and brutally murdered by officers of the Guards Cavalry Division. For the moment at least, at the price of all democratic principle, the Bolshevik menace had been suppressed. The nationwide elections proceeded on January 19, 1919, to elect delegates to a National Assembly for the framing of a constitution. The Social Democrats received 13 million votes. The centrist parties, representing the middle classes and the Catholic interests, received 11.5 million votes. The conservative parties, ranging from industrial conservatives to outright reactionaries and monarchists, received over 4.5 million votes. Thus the National Assembly which met in the small city of Weimar on February 6, 1919, hardly represented a revolutionary force in German affairs. Nevertheless, the delegates dutifully proceeded to produce a constitution for the new German Republic, which turned out to be technically the most democratic in the world—on paper. Political power was declared to reside only in the sovereign people; equality for all before the law was ensured; even a system of proportional representation was instituted to assure minorities a voice in the new Reichstag. Germany would be ruled by a cabinet and chancellor elected by majority vote in, and responsible to, the Reichstag. The head of state would be a president elected by the whole nation, whose powers would be severely limited. However, among these severely limited powers was the right to suspend civil liberties for stated periods of time if this should prove necessary.

The terms of the Treaty of Versailles were publicly printed in Berlin on May 7, 1919, while the Weimar

Assembly was debating the new constitution. Germans seemed to have forgotten that they had lost a great war and that the peace treaty would reflect this fact. In any event, a great wave of outrage swept over the country when the terms became known. The treaty provided for the return of Alsace-Lorraine to France (Bismarck had grabbed it in 1870), the return of those parts of Schleswig-Holstein seized from Denmark, and the turning over of certain Polish-inhabited lands in the east, including the provinces of Posen and Upper Silesia, to the new Polish state. The German Army was to be restricted to 100,000 volunteers and stripped of offensive weapons such as tanks and planes. The Great General Staff was to be outlawed. Reparations—German payment for war costs and damages—were to be established later. And, finally, by signing the treaty, Germany was to accept article #231, which stated: "The Allied Governments affirm and Germany accepts the responsibility of Germany and her Allies for causing all the loss and damage . . . [caused by] . . . the aggression of Germany and her Allies." In other words, Germany was to admit herself an aggressor nation who had caused the great war.

Germans united in outraged denunciation of the Treaty of Versailles. The National Assembly at Weimar declared it unacceptable. In later years it was to be used as an excuse for German revenge. Yet the treaty was by no means so harsh as the Treaty of Brest-Litovsk, which the victorious Germans had imposed upon the defeated Russians in 1917-18. Nevertheless, Ebert and his associates were prepared to reject it, provided the General Staff and the Army would support them. But Hindenburg and Groener both knew that any renewal of resistance to the Allies was militarily hopeless; they advised the National Assembly to swallow the bitter pill. Accordingly, on June 28, 1919, German representatives signed the Treaty of Versailles in the Hall of Mirrors in the Palace at Versailles, where fifty years earlier the German Empire had been proclaimed. And for this humiliation the German people did not blame the General Staff and the Army, which had been so largely responsible for it; instead they blamed the new republican government. Not only that, but they even swallowed the lie, put abroad by Ludendorff and other generals, that the German Army had not in fact been defeated on the field of battle, but rather "stabbed in the back" by politicians, businessmen, Bolsheviks, and speculators on the home front.

The Weimar Constitution was approved by the Assembly on July 31, 1919, and the new republican German government took up its duties in Berlin under President Friedrich Ebert.

In the chaotic winter of 1918-19, Adolf Hitler, discharged from the hospital at Pasewalk, first did a tour of duty guarding prisoners of war at Traunstein (near the Austrian border) and then went to Munich to try his luck.

There he wangled himself a job as a political propagandist—a "political education officer"—with the Army in Munich. His job was to lecture soldiers on the dangers of democracy, socialism, and disobedience, while at the same time he acted as a sort of official informer for the Army to spy out and report on the activity of suspicious political groups in the city. It was in this capacity that he was sent one evening in September 1919 to observe and then report on one of the meetings of a small group calling itself the German Workers' party—evidently the use of the word "workers" in the party title being deemed sufficiently suspicious to warrant investigation. Hitler, who was bored with the meeting, which was attended by about two dozen people gathered in a beer cellar, was about to leave when an elderly professor arose to criticize the reactionary viewpoints expressed by the party committee during the meeting. Moved to fury by the professor's remarks, Hitler harangued the meeting for half an hour. Then the professor departed ("like a wet poodle," according to Hitler), and one of the party leaders (Hitler could not recall his name) handed him some leaflets and begged him to join the party.

At first Hitler was skeptical. Although in many ways the German Workers' party reflected his own views, it seemed a ridiculously small and badly organized group to offer scope to his ambitions. But after a few days' reflection he realized that its very smallness would enable him to dominate it, while he had few doubts of his ability to build it into an effective instrument of personal power. At the next meeting Adolf Hitler was enrolled as the seventh member of the German Workers' party executive committee.

The German Workers' party had been founded a few years earlier by one Anton Drexler, a sickly, uneducated, bitter man (he was a locksmith by trade) whose aim it was to combat Marxism by offering the workers socialism as a function of extreme nationalism. The muddy social-economic ideas of Drexler and his handful of followers, if not to be described as simple opportunism, could perhaps be called a primitive form of state capitalism. Needless to say, racism, anti-Semitism, militarism, and plain hatred born of personal frustration were the real bases of the German Workers' party.

Hitler, who was thirty years old when he joined the German Workers' party, threw himself into its work with an energy he had never before displayed but which was to be characteristic of him from now on. He forced the executive committee to call larger and more frequent meetings, wrote party propaganda leaflets, addressed envelopes, undertook any and every task which would help build the party following. But above all he addressed meetings. For if Adolf Hitler had displayed few talents in his life up to then, he now discovered himself to be a fantastically effective orator. The emotional range of his voice, which could leap from rage to hysterical sorrow within a single sentence, the harsh gutturals of his Austrian accent, the instinctive rhythm with which he pounded home his ideas—these constituted a truly remarkable weapon and one which he learned to exploit masterfully. The power of Hitler's oratory, the emotional impact of his voice—which was slightly comic to foreign ears—had a sensationally effective, almost hypnotic effect on German audiences and constituted one of his greatest weapons in the struggle for power.

It was not long before the violent energy and peculiar fanaticism of the newest member of the party's executive committee brought real control of the party into his hands. It was his idea to add the words "National Socialist" to the party's name, so that it became, in the summer of 1920, the National Socialist German Workers' party—or, for short in German, the Nazi party. It was his idea to organize some of the roughnecks in the party into squads of strong-arm thugs to protect party meetings and, later, to break up meetings of opposition groups. These bands of rowdies (largely recruited from among Free Corps men) were given the name *Sturmabteilung* (Storm Battalion) on October 5, 1921, and later came to be known by the initials SA —the Stormtroopers. It was Hitler too who chose the party symbol—the swastika (卐). This sign of the hooked cross was very ancient—it can be found as far east as India amid the ruins of long-vanished civilizations. Possibly because of its antique association with India, whence in ages gone by the Indo-European Aryan races were supposed to have sprung, according to popular German myth, the symbol was already a popular one with German nationalists when Hitler chose it. In any event it seemed to exert an almost

mystical spell over the German mind when it sprouted
on flags, uniforms, armbands, and all the paraphernalia of nazidom.

By the summer of 1921, Hitler had made himself
the absolute and undisputed master of the National Socialist German Workers' party. And if many of its former chiefs had resigned in disgust, the party now had a
much larger following among the people (although it
was still relatively small) and a much larger treasury.
The money with which the party conducted its work at
this time came from two basic sources: from collections made at meetings and private donations by party
members; and from funds probably secretly supplied
by the German Army. For in this new party and its
fiery young leader the local German Army chiefs were
beginning to see great promise. Here was a party and a
man who seemed able to enlist the sympathy of masses
of workers for a program of extreme nationalism and
repression. One of the original members of the old
German Workers' party had been Captain Ernst
Roehm, an officer of the Army's District Command
VII and a leader among the ferocious Free Corps men
in Munich. It was through Roehm that the local Army
command from time to time advanced money to the
Free Corps, and it was through him that they also advanced money to the fledgling Nazi party. Roehm, a
thick-necked, scar-faced professional soldier, was a notorious homosexual but an effective organizer. It was
he who first organized the SA detachments for the
party and who built these Stormtroopers into a huge
private army over the next decade. In December of
1920 it was most probably through Captain Ernst
Roehm that the Nazi party found the funds necessary
to purchase a run-down local newspaper—the *Voelkischer Beobachter* (People's Guardian)—which became the party's official propaganda organ and under
its new management greatly increased its circulation.

Many of the men who were to rise to command in Nazi Germany joined Hitler during these early years. Rudolf Hess, who was to become Hitler's heir (until 1940) joined the party in 1920. A dull-witted but doggedly loyal young man of no particular ability, he had been raised in Egypt, where his father was a wholesale merchant, educated in Germany, wounded twice during World War I (he transferred from infantry to air force in 1918 and learned to fly), and been involved in Free Corps activity since 1919. He quickly became one of Hitler's most adoring followers, submerging his own thin personality in that of his beloved leader.

Alfred Rosenberg, although he was later to become the Nazi party's chief "philosopher," also was a man of low intelligence. He had been born and raised and educated in Russia, graduating from Moscow University with a degree in architecture in 1917. He lived through the Bolshevik Revolution in Russia but did not join it. Instead he joined the Germany Army in 1918. After the war he made his way to Munich, met Hitler, and joined the Nazi party in 1919. Later, in 1923, Hitler was to make him editor of the *Voelkischer Beobachter,* where his muddled opinions found expression in endless columns of turgid prose.

Hermann Goering, who joined the Nazi party after meeting Hitler in 1921, was a recruit of much larger stature (physically, as well as politically, as his ever-expanding girth demonstrated). A hero of World War I, he had been the last commander of the renowned Richthofen Fighter Squadron and held the "Pour le Mérite," Germany's highest wartime decoration. Married to a Swedish heiress, Goering was able to contribute heavily to the party's shaky finances and helped Roehm to organize the SA. Later he was to expend his considerable energies on the reconstruction of the German Air Force and become, until the last days of

World War II, the second most powerful man in Nazi Germany.

And these early years brought lesser-known personalities into the Nazi party too. There was Max Amann, Hitler's first sergeant during the war, who was made financial director of the party; Ulrich Graf, an amateur wrestler who became Hitler's personal bodyguard; Heinrich Hoffmann, who became official party photographer and the only man permitted to take photos of Hitler; Ernst (Putzi) Hanfstaengl, the half-American Harvard graduate whose clowning and piano playing made him for years Hitler's favorite court fool; and there was Julius Streicher, a half-crazed sadist and pornographer whose weekly magazine, *Der Stuermer,* specialized in the most perverted type of anti-Semitism.

In April of 1921 the Allied governments handed Germany a bill for War Reparations in the amount of $33 billion. While Germans of every political stripe protested that they could not possibly pay such an amount, the German mark rapidly lost its value. Over a period of two years it slipped from less than 4 marks on the dollar to 400 marks to the dollar, and its purchasing power within Germany declined correspondingly. The republican government in Berlin asked the Allies for a postponement of reparations payments. But the French government refused to allow this, and when Germany defaulted on payments, the French Army marched into the Ruhr, Germany's great industrial region, in January of 1923. Thereupon the value of the mark fell to 18,000 to the dollar.

But, while German workers reacted to the French occupation of the Ruhr with a very effective general strike, and the Army organized sabotage in the Ruhr industries, both the republican government and the industrialists realized that inflation might be the answer to their problems. With the mark almost worthless, German industrialists were able to repay indebtedness with nearly meaningless money, while the government could make reparations payments in equally cheap coin. Furthermore, inflation was another weapon against the hated French in the Ruhr. So the republican government and the financial interests in Germany encouraged the fall of the mark. By August of 1923 it took 4 billion marks to buy one dollar, and thereafter the figures climbed into the trillions.

But what benefited German capitalists was a disaster to the German people. With their currency worthless, Germans found their salaries and wages reduced to zero in purchasing power. Life savings were wiped out, bank accounts turned into useless paper. It took billions of marks to buy a head of lettuce, hundreds of thousands of marks to purchase a few potatoes. What good was an economic system which brought such disaster to the people? And, above all, who was responsible for this catastrophe? The people (with, as we have seen, some justification) blamed the Republic. But beyond this they blamed democracy. Overlooking the large profits which industrialists and other capitalists made out of the inflation, the German people blamed their daily hunger and the ruin of their economy on the Weimar Republic. By November of 1923 the chaos and misery of German life was such that Adolf Hitler felt his hour had come. He prepared to strike.

Three

BEER HALL TO REICHSTAG

THE TRIGGER THAT TOUCHED OFF HITLER'S FIRST attempt to seize power was the decision by the republican government in Berlin, now headed by Chancellor Gustav Stresemann (since August 1923), to put an end to passive resistance against the French in the Ruhr and to resume payment of reparations. This policy of cooperation with the French would, Stresemann knew, be violently opposed by rightists. Anticipating that Bavaria, largely in the control of monarchist and Nazi fanatics, might attempt to set itself up as an independent state, Stresemann attempted to forestall such action by having President Ebert declare a state of emergency on September 26, 1923.

In Munich the news of Stresemann's policy of cooperation with the Allies produced just the reaction the Berlin government feared. On September 26 the Bavarian Cabinet proclaimed its own state of emergency and appointed Gustav von Kahr as State Commissioner with dictatorial powers. Kahr, as was well known, was dedicated to a return of the local Bavarian monarchy. Sharing his defiance of the Berlin authorities were Colonel Hans von Seisser, Chief of the Bavarian State Police and General Otto von Lossow, Commander of the German Army forces in Bavaria. These three men assumed control of the Bavarian state and refused to obey orders from Berlin. When Berlin issued a plain warning that the Army would suppress by force any attempt to organize a rebellion, the Bavarian ministers ignored it.

If Adolf Hitler was now presented with an opportunity to act, he was also faced with a grave problem. He had learned long ago in Vienna that a political party which hoped to seize power in the state must count on the support of the Army and a few other established institutions. Although anxious to lead the Bavarian rebellion, he had no desire to bring himself and the Nazi party into conflict with the German Army; that, he saw, would be disastrous. Besides that, he did not share von Kahr's love of the old Bavarian monarchy nor the desire to set up an independent Bavarian state. Hitler's whole policy aimed at a monolithic, united Germany in which local independence was inconceivable. On the other hand, Hitler felt himself trapped. For years now he had been rabidly denouncing the Berlin government, whipping up his followers into paroxysms of hatred against the Republic. These followers were now demanding action. If Hitler refused to act, they might well desert the Nazi party in favor of some other organization which *was* prepared to act. Besides, there was just a slim chance that the rebellion might succeed in spite of everything. If Hitler could first gain control of the Bavarian government, then succeed in winning the support of the Army units in Bavaria, he might be able to raise a nationwide revolt against the German Republic. And to gain the support of local Army units Hitler had, as his ace in the hole, the backing of General Erich Ludendorff, the legendary Commander in Chief of World War I. Surely the Army could be counted on to back their wartime leader. The situation, as Hitler saw it, called for boldness and daring—qualities which he now proved he had.

In order to gain control of the Bavarian government, Hitler and the Nazi leaders decided to kidnap its leaders and force them at gunpoint to acknowledge Hitler's leadership and the Nazi program. Several plots were hatched to accomplish this, but on each occasion chance placed obstacles in Hitler's path—until November 8, 1923. On that day it was announced that von Kahr, General von Lossow, and Colonel von Seisser would address a gathering of businessmen at the Buergerbraukeller (a local beer cellar) in the evening. The opportunity to catch all three Bavarian leaders in one net could not be missed.

At nine o'clock in the evening, after von Kahr had been addressing his audience of three thousand businessmen for about an hour, hundreds of Nazi SA troops, under the command of Hermann Goering, surrounded the beer cellar. While some of the troops set up a machine gun at the entrance Hitler pushed into the cellar waving a pistol.

"The National Revolution has begun!" he shouted to the astounded audience. The building was occupied by six hundred heavily armed men, he warned. No one would be allowed to leave the hall. The Bavarian and Reich governments had been removed . . . the Army and the police were marching on Munich under the swastika banner!

These were all, of course, pure lies. But the bluff worked. While the amazed businessmen gazed uneasily at the SA thugs gathered in the hall Hitler ordered von Kahr, General von Lossow, and Colonel von Seisser into a back room. There, waving his pistol in their faces, he demanded that they join him in declaring a nationwide revolution, in leading a march on Berlin.

But the three men disdainfully refused. In fact they refused even to speak to Hitler.

He had four shots in his pistol! Hitler cried. Three for them if they abandoned him, the last bullet for himself. But the three men who held the power in the Bavarian state greeted these words with contempt.

Suddenly, on inspiration, Hitler dashed from the room, mounted the rostrum in the beer cellar and shouted to the assembled throng that von Kahr, Lossow, and Seisser had agreed to join him! It was, to be sure, a very big and very bald lie, but it worked. The assembled businessmen and SA troopers cheered wildly. Within the locked side room the Bavarian leaders were impressed. They were even more impressed when General Ludendorff appeared. The general, who had had no foreknowledge of Hitler's plan, had been routed out of bed and hurried to the beer cellar. Although he was angry at Hitler for this undignified procedure, he now willingly supported the uprising. He advised von Kahr, von Lossow, and von Siesser to go along with Hitler. Overawed by the general's presence, impressed by the sound of cheering, and aware of their probable fate should they refuse, the three men capitulated. They swore loyalty to each other and to the rebellion before the cheering businessmen.

Hitler, in raptures, now decided he could safely leave the beer cellar in order to attend to other steps in his plan. But this was a fatal mistake. Once the Nazi leader had left the place, von Kahr, von Lossow, and von Seisser found it easy to talk Ludendorff into letting them go. When Hitler returned, his captives had fled. Dismayed by this, Hitler was further horrified to find that nothing else in his plan was going right. No one was marching on Munich, none of the government buildings except the Army headquarters had been seized (Ernst Roehm and a small band of SA men were holed up there), and it was soon apparent that the local Army units were prepared to follow the orders, not of General Ludendorff, but of General von Seeckt in Berlin. By dawn regular Army troops marched into Munich and sealed off Roehm's SA men in the war Ministry. Furthermore, von Kahr, von Lossow, and von Seisser had moved the Bavarian government to nearby Regensburg and issued a proclamation denouncing Hitler and retracting their promises made, as they pointed out, under duress. The plot, it seemed, had gone to pieces.

But General Ludendorff now proposed to Hitler a new plan which might bring success after all. German soldiers and policemen, the general was sure, would never fire on him—their former war leader. So he and Hitler and their followers would simply march into the center of Munich and take over the city. The Army and police would, he was certain, accept his orders. Hitler was skeptical but agreed. He had nothing to lose now.

At about eleven o'clock on the morning of November 9, Hitler and Ludendorff, along with Goering, Rosenberg, and Ulrich Graf (Hitler's bodyguard), behind the swastika banner and leading a column of about five hundred heavily armed Stormtroopers, marched into the center of Munich. Their objective was to relieve Ernst Roehm and his SA men still besieged at the War Ministry. But they never got there.

For just as they neared their destination, as they were passing through a very narrow street known as the Residenzstrasse, a group of about one hundred rifle-carrying policemen appeared to block their way. Hitler and Ludendorff tried to talk their way through the police lines. But in spite of Ludendorff's presence, the police stood firm. Someone—it was never established who—fired a shot. Immediately the police opened fire. Volley after volley crashed down the Residenzstrasse. The man standing next to Hitler fell, mortally wounded. His arm had been linked in Hitler's and his fall dragged the Nazi leader abruptly to the pavement, the impact dislocating Hitler's shoulder. Although the firing lasted only one minute, sixteen Nazis were killed as well as three policemen. The rest of the Nazis clutched the pavement along with Hitler. Only General Ludendorff remained standing. Contemptuous both of police bullets and his Nazi associates, the old general continued to walk stolidly ahead—through the police lines—until he arrived alone at his destination, where he was promptly arrested.

Hitler meantime had scampered to safety, leaping into a nearby automobile which carried him to the country house of the Hanfstaengls. Goering likewise made good his escape over the Austrian frontier. But within a matter of days Hitler and some of the other top Nazi leaders were arrested and, on February 26, 1924, along with Ludendorff, were put on trial for treason in Munich.

The trial, which was a news sensation throughout Germany, gave Hitler the opportunity to be heard beyond the confines of Bavaria for the first time. The assembled newspapermen reported his words the length and breadth of the Fatherland and, by the time the trial ended, Hitler was a national figure. For Hitler, allowed to dominate the courtroom by the sympathetic judges, turned his treason trial into a propaganda victory.

Yes, he admitted in the first of his many long speeches to the court, that was what he'd *wanted* to do: to destroy the State. He alone bore the responsibility, but he was not a criminal because of that. There was no such thing as high treason against the traitors of 1918. He knew, he said, what the verdict of the court would be, but history would give another verdict. And if he was guilty, so were such men as Kahr and Lossow and Seisser, who also had plotted rebellion.

After consuming days in endless harangues which outlined the Nazi philosophy, Hitler in his closing address to the court declared: "I believe that the hour will come when the masses, who today stand in the street with our swastika banner, will unite with those who fired upon them. . . . One day the hour will come when the Army will stand at our side, officers and men." It was to prove a tragically accurate prediction.

The judges, men who had been hand-picked by a Nazi sympathizer in the Bavarian government, returned their verdict on April 1, 1924. They acquitted General Ludendorff, doled out very mild sentences to the other defendants, and ordered Hitler himself imprisoned for five years—which meant that he would be eligible for parole in six months. Furthermore, his imprisonment was made as comfortable as possible. He was assigned a private and spacious room in the old Landsberg fortress with a fine view, received gifts and visitors whenever he wished, and was even permitted to employ his fellow prisoner Rudolf Hess as a private secretary. For during the period of his imprisonment (he was to be released nine months later, on December 1, 1924), Adolf Hitler decided to devote himself to dictating a book which would record his rise to prominence and serve as a blueprint for the future of his movement. The title, suggested to him by Max Amann, the Nazi party financial director, was *Mein Kampf* (My Battle).

If *Mein Kampf* made difficult and unappetizing reading (even the most fervent Nazis admitted that the book was heavy going—few ever read it through), it was certainly a direct statement of Hitler's plans. Much of it was devoted to a rehashing of the muddled ideas Hitler had gained from his imperfect understanding of the nineteenth-century German philosophers. Much of it was pure hysteria. But certain of Hitler's attitudes and plans which were to form the basis of the Nazi government and of his foreign policy were frankly stated for all the world to read. The fact that only a handful of people outside Germany ever took *Mein Kampf* seriously was a tragic mistake for the entire world.

German policy, as outlined by Hitler, was to be based on three factors. First was the reorganization of German life on the Leadership principle. This meant that supreme power in the German state was to be exercised by one man (himself, of course), while on every level of German life lesser leaders responsible only to those above them were to have absolute authority. Thus a chain of absolute command would be created to permeate all aspects of German life. The second principle was that of the purity and superiority of the German race. To purify this race, Jews and other non-Germans were to be "eliminated" from German national life. Intermarriage between Germans and non-Germans, especially Jews, was to become a crime. The other races of the world must be made slaves of the superrace of Germans or wiped out. The third principle was that of foreign conquest and domination. Germany deserved to rule all Europe—in fact, all the world—due to its innate racial superiority. This would be accomplished first by destroying the power of the Western Allies—notably France—and then conquering the Slavs in the east. Thus a vast territory would be carved out for Germany to expand into. Then, with secure domination of the European continent, German power could reach out for world conquest.

Sane people outside Germany might laugh at these ridiculous and grandiose posturings of the absurd little man with the Charlie Chaplin mustache, but one thing was certain: Hitler would put his ideas into operation ruthlessly if ever he came into control of the German nation.

By the time he left Landsberg Prison, on December

1, 1924, Adolf Hitler had some revised plans to achieve that end—and the same blind faith in his own powers, his destiny, to succeed. And he was to be helped on his road to power by those too blind to see that he actually meant what he said.

First of all, Hitler had come to the conclusion that it was necessary to reorganize the Nazi party completely and along different lines. Many years later he explained: "We recognized that it is not enough to overthrow the old state, but that the new state must previously have been built up and be practically ready to one's hand. . . . In 1933 it was no longer a question of overthrowing a state by an act of violence; meanwhile the new state had been built up and all that there remained to do was to destroy the last remnants of the old state—and that took but a few hours."

What the building up of a new state—a state-within-in-a-state—meant was amply demonstrated over the next few years. Beginning in 1925, the Nazi party was divided into two groups known as PO I and PO II. PO I was devoted to the undermining and overthrow of the German state; PO II was designed to provide that new state-within-a-state which Hitler now desired. Departments of Agriculture, Justice, Economy, Interior, Labor, Race, Culture, Foreign Affairs, Propaganda, and others were established, which functioned (or pretended to function) just as the real government departments functioned. The country was divided into thirty-four districts, or *Gaue*—each with its leader and party structure down to block level (in the cities). Separate organizations were created for young people —the Hitler Youth (which specialized in "defense sports" as well as Boy Scout activities); for housewives, lawyers, students, teachers, doctors—all had their separate groups and clubs. The roughneck Sturmabteilung, the SA, was reorganized into an armed band of several hundred thousand men who specialized in terrorizing the defenseless, breaking up meetings of Hitler's opponents, and protecting Nazi party meetings. And besides this mob of brawlers, Hitler now organized a group of thugs for his personal bodyguard. They were called Schutzstaffel, or SS, men and were dressed in black shirts in imitation of Mussolini's Fascists. Much more disciplined than the SA and more directly dependent upon Hitler personally, the SS slowly grew over the years into formidable numbers. But it was not until 1929 that Hitler found an ideal commander for this group in the person of one Heinrich Himmler, a quiet, seemingly mild-mannered chicken farmer from Bavaria. But behind the spectacled face, which looked like that of a schoolteacher, Heinrich Himmler's personality was that of a homicidal maniac.

Hitler's second important decision after leaving Landsberg Prison was that the Nazi party would henceforth pursue its ends only by constitutional means. It would achieve power by winning the votes of a majority of the German people. Of course, how these votes were won might include political assassination, smear campaigns, massive lies, bribery—all the catalog of politically immoral actions—but technically they would be aimed at a purely constitutional victory at the polls. There would be no more attempts at outright rebellion. For Hitler understood that a dictatorship must come to power with the real or apparent support of a majority of the people in order to win the vital support of established institutions such as the Army, or industry, or the Church.

The growth of the Nazi party during the twenties was slow at first. In 1925 there were 27,000 dues-paying members; in 1926, 49,000; in 1927, 72,000; in 1928, 108,000; in 1929, 178,000. In the national elections of 1924 (held while Hitler was in prison) a Nazi front party supported by Ludendorff polled only 2 million votes and elected (thanks to the system of proportional representation, which assured any minority of representation) only 32 deputies to the Reichstag. Hitler had been against entering candidates in the election, but while he enjoyed the hospitality of Landsberg Prison a young man named Gregor Strasser, who had risen suddenly to the front rank of Nazi leaders, had organized the election effort. A former druggist, and a Bavarian, Strasser was an independent-minded man who took the "socialism" in national socialism entirely too seriously for Hitler's taste. Nevertheless, recognizing Strasser's immense energy and real organizing capabilities, Hitler assigned him the task of organizing the Nazi party in the north—especially in Prussia and in Berlin. To help him in his work, Strasser enlisted the support of a 28-year-old Rhinelander named Paul Josef Goebbels. Goebbels, a physically small individual with a lame left leg, was one of the few Nazi leaders to have had a thorough education. He attended eight of Germany's finest universities before gaining his Ph.D. in philosophy from Heidelberg in 1921. He was an eloquent speaker and a fervent Nazi with a special flair for propaganda (*i.e.*, lying). Although originally raised to prominence in the movement by Gregor Strasser and, like Strasser, a believer in "socialism," Goebbels soon fell under Hitler's spell, deserted his former patron, and became Hitler's most devoted follower.

If, in spite of Hitler's plans, the progress of nazism was slow through the twenties, the basic reason for this could be found in the progress made by the republican government in Berlin. Under the leadership of Gustav Stresemann, the German Republic had gained Allied acceptance of a revision of reparations policy. The American financier Charles G. Dawes drew up a plan whereby German reparations were much reduced and the German mark stabilized. The Dawes Plan, which was accepted by the Allies on August 16, 1924, was even more important in that it ensured American financial investment in the rebuilding of German industry. From 1924 until 1932 American investment in Germany amounted to nearly $7 billion and was no small factor in the upsurge of German prosperity during the twenties.

Stresemann's policies, though opposed by German extremists, were generally supported by the Social Democrats, who continued to be the largest party in the Reichstag, and at first by the Communists. The crushing of the Spartacist movement during the chaotic days of 1919 had by no means put an end to Communist influence among the German workers; if anything, the savage repression increased that influence. But the German Communist party was largely a captive of Russian policy, and in the years after 1923 that meant a captive of Stalin's personal policy. And, although nazism was communism's most obvious and direct enemy, Stalin, who was busily purging Russian life of his real and imagined enemies, saw more of a threat to his personal power in the activities of Socialists and Social Democrats, be they Russian or German. So although Communist and Nazi street gangs maintained a running minor civil war all through the late twenties and early thirties, the German Communist party's official policy was to destroy the Social Democrats and Socialists first, even at the price of allying themselves with Nazis during crucial votes in the Reichstag.

Another source of support for Stresemann's policies during the prosperous years from 1923 to 1929 was the German Army. This ancient state-within-a-state was devoted to one primary aim—the preservation of its own privileged existence as a basis for future expansion. Under the command of General Hans von Seeckt, the German Army exerted force in German political life only when political upheaval threatened its own plans or discipline—as in the case of the Beer Hall *Putsch* of 1923. By the Treaty of Versailles the

German Army had been reduced to 100,000 men, modern equipment and planes denied it, and the General Staff abolished. Furthermore, the Allied Military Control Commission was in Berlin to oversee the carrying out of these treaty obligations.

Seeckt overcame the Allied decree abolishing the General Staff by the simple expedient of changing its name to the Troop Office, and scattering some of its officers among German divisions of lower echelons. But General Staff teaching, doctrine, and planning continued beneath these thin disguises. The reduction of the German Army to 100,000 men made German defense of her eastern frontiers very difficult against the renewed power of Polish nationalism. But here Seeckt used the freebooting, non-Army Free Corps, which was soon organized in the east into a secret "Black" Army. Supplies for these groups were hidden on the great Junker estates of Prussia, and General Staff officers dressed in civilian clothes were assigned to guide them. But while these developments might be hidden from the Allied Control Commission, the introduction of new weapons into the German Army and the rebuilding of an Air Force could not. Therefore, General Seeckt made a number of secret agreements with the Red Army. Thus it was agreed that the Red Army would receive instruction in General Staff techniques and doctrine from German General Staff officers; German officers would be permitted to observe Russian Army maneuvers in order to gain first-hand experience in the use of new weapons and techniques. More than that, Russian factories, financed and engineered by Germans, were set up outside Moscow and other industrial centers for the production of German tanks and German planes. German pilots trained with the Red Air Force and German specialists—from paratroopers to tank corps men—received practical experience on the Russian maneuver fields.

It will be seen, then, that the forces of reaction and conquest were not dead in Germany from 1923 to 1929—they were merely disguised. Behind the republican front, industrialists, the Army, the Communists, the fanatic right led more and more by Hitler's Nazis, were busily digging the grave of the republican government. In February 1925 that government had itself undergone a change of face. In that year the old trade unionist and first President of the Republic, Friedrich Ebert, had died. Fearful of the possible coming to power of either a Communist or a Nazi as president, the middle-of-the-road and conservative parties united to back Field Marshal Paul von Hindenburg, the aging hero of World War I. It was his face—heavy, sleepy, dignified, honorable—which the rest of the world saw as the image of the new republican Germany thereafter. As for the busy fanatic Adolf Hitler, he was slightly comic and relatively unimportant. His reorganized Nazi party polled only 810,000 votes in 1928 and elected only 12 deputies to the Reichstag. To most Germans he remained a joke.

The joke, however, ceased to be funny on October 29, 1929. That was the day the Stock Market crashed in New York to signal the start of worldwide depression. The results in Germany were drastic. German prosperity had been based on American loans and world trade. But now the flow of loans abruptly ceased and payment on old loans was urgently demanded. The German financial structure could not stand the strain and collapsed. Banks failed throughout Germany and Austria. Once again life savings were wiped out, and the specter of renewed inflation swept the country. And with the collapse of the world economic market, German exports—the lifeblood of the German economy—were almost completely wiped out. Industrial enterprises closed their gates, the great Ruhr manufacturers cut back production to a mere trickle, and small businesses throughout Germany collapsed. Unemployment skyrocketed and poverty, misery, and starvation stalked the land once again.

After he came to power in 1933, Hitler once gloated: "We are the result of the distress for which the others are responsible." And certainly the Great Depression, which brought misery to so many, brought golden opportunity to the Nazis. Hitler wrote that never in his life had he been so well-disposed and inwardly contented as in those days. For hard reality was opening the eyes of millions of Germans to the "unprecedented swindles, lies and betrayals" of the "Marxist deceivers of the people." Of course Hitler, with only the crudest understanding of economics, had no more idea than anyone else what had really caused the depression—nor did he care. He saw only the 6 million unemployed who demanded work, the millions of youths who demanded some sort of secure future, the hundreds of thousands of small shopkeepers and artisans whose livelihood had been obliterated, and the great industrialists and bankers who now more than ever feared a Communist uprising. Fear, insecurity, despair—these were the strands with which Hitler now proceeded to weave a web of power.

With the Social Democrats, although still the largest party, unable to provide a program that would win acceptance by the Reichstag, President von Hindenburg scheduled new elections for September 14, 1930.

Immediately, Adolf Hitler recognized a heaven-sent (as he put it) opportunity. He organized a whirlwind political campaign with the help of Goebbels, Strasser, and his thousands of fanatically devoted followers. To the unemployed he promised work, to the failed small businessmen he promised prosperity, to the industrialists he promised profits. And all these apparently contradictory ends were to be achieved as a natural outgrowth of the Nazi program. Germany must be made strong again, the Treaty of Versailles torn up, payment of further reparations refused. A militaristic policy would provide jobs, reopen factories, bring prosperity—by a tremendous expansion of the armaments industry, by the drafting of millions into a new German Army, by government manipulation of credit and finance. To the despairing, Hitler painted his dream of Germany restored to splendor—where all other symbols seemed to be failing, he offered the new symbol of the swastika. To the embittered and fearful he offered his pet hate, the Jews, as a national scapegoat.

On September 14, 1930, the Nazi party received nearly 6.5 million votes in the national elections. The Nazis returned 107 deputies to the Reichstag. Although the Social Democrats remained the majority party in Germany, although the Communists polled 4.5 million votes, it was suddenly and stunningly clear that nazism was a success among a huge mass of the German people. The Nazi party, now the second largest in the Reichstag, had overnight become a power to reckon with, and the comic little man from Munich was no longer funny.

Now, for the first time, those ancient pillars of German life—the Army and many industrialists—began to see in the Nazi movement a means whereby mass support might be won for their own programs. Here was a man who could win popular support for a program to crush communism, socialism, trade-unionism: all those movements which seemed to threaten the rich and powerful. Millions of marks were donated to the Nazi party by certain German industrialists following personal meetings with Hitler.

Successful in dealing with Germany's industrial magnates, Hitler now applied himself to winning the support of the German Army. At the trial in Leipzig of three junior officers who were charged with membership in the Nazi party Hitler appeared as a witness. In his usual fashion he used the courtroom as a soapbox. Speaking for the ears of Army officers throughout Germany, he declared that he had always believed that any attempt to replace the Army would be madness. He would see to it, Hitler promised, when he came to power, that a great Army of the German people would arise. The Army heard, and, like the industrialists and businessmen, the German Army now came to believe that Hitler could be used to further its own ends.

The central fact of the months between September 1930 and January 1933 was that no government could successfully rule Germany that did not have Nazi support, and few men could be found who would risk presiding over a government which included Nazis. Field Marshal von Hindenburg, now in his eighties and falling more and more into the senility of old age, was to many the last bulwark against the rising power of the Nazi party. Much against his will, the old President (he was eighty-five) agreed to run again for the presidency in 1932. His principal opponents in the election were to be Hitler and his Nazi party, and the Communists (who even at this late date were more interested in destroying their left-wing enemies than in uniting with them to destroy Hitler), whose candidate was Ernst Thaelmann, the party's leader.

Hitler waged his usual energetic campaign. As always he ran against the Treaty of Versailles, the Jews, the "November 1918 traitors," and other simple-minded fictions he had erected into scarecrows to deceive the stupid. His efforts were rewarded on April 10, 1932, when the final election results showed that, although Hindenburg had received more than 19 million votes, a clear majority, and Thaelmann had received almost 4 million votes, the Nazis and their candidate had won almost 13.5 million votes—an indication of mass support which could no longer be ignored.

After a series of crises and plots, which grew in desperation throughout the last months of 1932 and which only reflected the complete chaos and impotence of the German government, President von Hindenburg, by January 1933, found himself left with no alternative but to summon Adolf Hitler to become Chancellor of Germany. But by then the move was almost an anticlimax.

For all during the last years of the Republic the Nazi organizations—from Stormtroopers to Hitler Youth, from Culture Clubs to Propaganda Department —had flourished mightily. With the heavy Nazi vote of 1930, hundreds of thousands of new recruits had flocked to Hitler's swastika banner. Mass meetings attended by many thousands, guarded by the uniformed SA troops, decorated with the Roman Legion-type standards of the Nazi party (which had been personally designed by Hitler), at which Hitler, Goebbels, and their followers harangued the multitudes had become common spectacles in German life. The disruption of Reichstag proceedings on the part of the more than 100 Nazi deputies, often led by the brawling vulgarity of Hermann Goering, were predictable occurrences. The smashing of windows, cries, thud of fists, and occasional pistol shots as Stormtroopers battled anyone and everyone who opposed Hitler had become daily occurrences in every German town and city. The ever-widening stream of lies and hatred and filth poured out daily by such Nazi newspapers as the *Voelkischer Beobachter, Der Angriff,* and Julius Streicher's particularly foul *Der Stuermer* had become popular reading matter. It seemed that Hitler was a foreordained destiny for the German people—Field Marshal Walther von Brauchitsch, the Commander in Chief of the German Army from 1938 to 1941, later expressed this feeling: "Hitler was the fate of Germany, and this fate could not be stayed."

So on Monday, January 30, 1933, just before the noon hour, Adolf Hitler was called to the Chancellery for an interview with President von Hindenburg. To his followers who remained behind in the suite of rooms they had rented at Berlin's Kaiserhof Hotel the outcome of the interview was a foregone conclusion. Hermann Goering was certain Hitler would now be named Chancellor. Ernst Roehm, SA commander, and Rudolf Hess, Hitler's personal deputy, both agreed with Goering. Paul Goebbels, the party's Propaganda Chief, on the other hand, still had his doubts. "Our hearts are torn back and forth between doubt, hope, joy, and discouragement," Goebbels noted in his diary. "We have been disappointed too often to believe wholeheartedly in the great miracle." But he needn't have worried. Hitler returned to the Kaiserhof within the hour—as Germany's new Chancellor. He had had to accept representatives of other parties in his new Cabinet, but he and his followers all understood that real and supreme power in the German state now rested in their hands.

That night, for hours on end, thousands and thousands of Stormtroopers marched through Berlin to celebrate the Nazi victory. Their bands played the old German martial airs, their drums boomed, the tramp of their jackboots shook the pavement, while the thousands of flaming torches they carried gave them the appearance of some army marching out of the dark ages of human history. On the Wilhelmstrasse, at the windows of the Chancellery building, Adolf Hitler responded with his outstretched-arm salute as the guttural roar of *"Sieg Heil!"* (Hail victory!) resounded through the night. And the German crowds, in their thousands, cheered the marching Stormtroopers. If there were any among them who felt the forebodings which such a scene must have aroused in the breast of any sane or civilized human being, they were careful to keep their silence. On that night of January 30, 1933, Germany plunged happily, deliriously, joyfully into an abyss from which she has not yet fully emerged.

Four

EIN VOLK, EIN REICH, EIN FUEHRER!

THE SLOGAN, *One People, One Government, One Leader!* which had been the Nazi battle cry for many years, now became the program of the new Chancellor, Adolf Hitler. And the first step in that program was the elimination of political opposition to Der Fuehrer (The Leader) and his party. For, although Hitler was Chancellor, his Cabinet included men from various other reactionary and ultrarightist parties, such as Franz von Papen (the former Chancellor, now Vice-Chancellor), and in the Reichstag itself he was faced with 100 Communist deputies and 121 Social Democratic deputies. These men, these parties—relics of the already doomed Republic—would have to be eliminated as the first step in establishing an absolute Nazi dictatorship. Hitler solved the problem abruptly. As his first step—and to the horror of his non-Nazi colleagues in the Cabinet—Der Fuehrer, within 48 hours of taking office as Chancellor, called for new nationwide elections to the Reichstag to be held on March 5, 1933. He was confident of their outcome.

For now, for the first time (in the last free elections Germany was to know for nearly twenty years), the

Nazi party could use all the vast resources of the German government to win votes. Besides that, they were well-assured of the support of the Army and of big business interests (who poured money into Nazi party coffers). Paul Goebbels, the Propaganda Chief, was now able to use the state-run radio exclusively for Nazi broadcasts. Hermann Goering, who had first been elected in 1932 President of the Reichstag and Minister of the Interior for the state of Prussia, had under his control the Prussian police and the Geheime Staatspolizei (Secret State Police), better known by its abbreviated name: Gestapo. He soon had replaced republican police officials with officers drawn from the SA and the SS and issued orders to the police not to display hostility to the actions of the Stormtroopers. On the other hand, police were to show no mercy to "enemies of the state." These "enemies" turned out to be not only the Communists, whose meetings were forbidden and whose press was suppressed, but also Social Democrats, Catholics, and trade unions. Stormtroopers broke up election rallies and meetings of all these groups, beating and often murdering their leaders.

Then on the evening of February 27, 1933, a rumor spread through Berlin: the Reichstag was on fire! Skeptical Berliners, used to wild propaganda stunts, who rushed to the scene found that this time the rumors were true. The great building that housed the German Parliament was a mass of flames and the smoke from its burning rose to a giant pillar in the night sky. Hitler and Goebbels, interrupting a private dinner at Goebbels' home, had rushed to the spot. Goering was already there along with hundreds of firemen and police. To the head of the Gestapo, Rudolf Diels, Goering angrily claimed that this was a Communist crime; the beginning of a Communist revolution! There was not a minute to lose; every Communist official should be shot; every Communist deputy strung up that very night! Goering's words seemed to have some trace of the truth behind them. For the police had arrested one Marinus van der Lubbe, a half-witted Dutch Communist who admitted, even boasted of, having started the fire.

On the following day Hitler easily persuaded the alarmed Hindenburg to sign a decree whereby the government was empowered to suspend all civil rights, act outside the law, arrest and even execute suspicious persons—all for the protection of the state against the Communists. Immediately, thousands of Communists, Social Democrats, trade unionists, and liberals were arrested by the police and the Stormtroopers, carted off to prisons and police barracks and often beaten and tortured to death. The democratic press—non-Communist as well as Communist—was banned, and the democratic parties were effectively prevented from campaigning in the election. "Documents" forged to "prove" Communist plans to carry out a campaign of terror throughout Germany were "discovered" and broadcast to the people. With all the resources of the government the Nazis whipped up a nationwide hysteria designed to stampede and frighten the German people into voting exclusively for the Nazis in the March 5 elections.

The truth about the Reichstag fire only came out after Germany's defeat in the Second World War. It was planned by Goebbels and carried out under the supervision of Hermann Goering. An underground passageway led from Goering's official residence in Berlin to the nearby Reichstag. And through this tunnel one Karl Ernst, chief of the Berlin SA, led a small party of Stormtroopers who spread the chemicals and gasoline and ignited the blaze. A few days earlier, by an incredible but true coincidence, the SA had arrested Marinus van der Lubbe when he was overheard boasting that he would set the Reichstag afire. The Dutch half-wit was encouraged to proceed with his plans by the SA, who used his small attempt at arson as a front for their own large-scale efforts.

Although the trial of van der Lubbe (who was beheaded) turned out to be something of a fiasco for the Nazis, the hysteria and fear they had whipped up throughout Germany gained them and their extremist allies enough votes on March 5 to enable them to deal with the Reichstag (which assembled now in Berlin's Kroll Opera House). Although the Nazis, with 17,277,180 votes, still did not have a clear majority of the more than 38 million votes cast, by uniting with rightist extremists and by denying their seats to 181 Communists deputies (whose election in spite of all the terror directed against them was a reflection of great bravery), they were able to secure the two-thirds majority vote necessary to hand over supreme power in the German nation to Adolf Hitler. On March 23, 1933, with the Kroll Opera House surrounded by thousands of shouting Stormtroopers, the Reichstag turned over all its constitutional authority to Hitler. Thereafter, although the Reichstag met from time to time at Hitler's bidding, it was never more than a cheering society for Der Fuehrer.

Hitler used his new dictatorial powers quickly and ruthlessly. Between March 31 and April 7 the last flickerings of independence in the German states were extinguished. A series of decrees ended their centuries-old rights and privileges, thereby transforming Germany into a unitary state. Between May 3 and July 5, 1933, the German political parties went out of existence—all of them, from Social Democrats to archconservatives. On July 14 a law proclaimed that only the Nazi party was henceforth to be permitted in Germany and any attempt to form any other political grouping was a criminal offense. On May 2 the German trade unions were dissolved. Union headquarters were seized and union leaders were arrested throughout Germany. The labor movement was now reorganized by the Nazis under strict government control. Robert Ley, a drunken Nazi chemist from Cologne, was appointed head of a German Labor Front, which soon reduced German workers to a status little better than slavery. And if German businessmen and conservatives applauded these measures, they were soon alarmed by Hitler's take-over of all German financial institutions. On March 17, 1933, Hitler appointed Dr. Hjalmar Schacht as president of the Reichsbank, Germany's state banking institution. There Dr. Schacht, a financier of great ability, was to bend German finances to the task of rearmament and the ruthless exploitation of German industry for Nazi ends. And, finally, Paul Josef Goebbels was rewarded for his devoted adoration of Der Fuehrer by being named chief of a newly created Ministry of Propaganda and Popular Enlightenment—a post from which he exercised absolute control of German newspapers, radio, films, books, and magazines.

In spite of these measures, however, Hitler still faced a few obstacles on his road to absolute power. The name of his party was the National Socialist party —and vast masses of his followers, as well as certain key Nazi leaders, had always emphasized the socialist aims of national socialism. Of course these "socialist" aims had nothing to do with real socialism. Instead they had always been merely lies to lure unwary voters —and a promise to the Nazi riffraff that they would one day take over the belongings and wealth of the upper classes. Such Nazis as Ernst Roehm, the homosexual Commander of the SA, whose "socialism" was no more than personal greed, now began to clamor for a "second revolution" which would bring them into direct control of German industry, the landed estates of the Junkers, and the wealth of the German big business establishment. But Hitler had no intention of alienating his business and Army supporters. This difference between Hitler's true aims and his promises reflected a different idea of the role of the SA, which had always been a source of argument between Der Fuehrer and Ernst Roehm. Hitler had created the SA for purely political ends. It was simply to supply the ingredient of terror and bullying needed to discourage opposition political parties. But to Ernst Roehm the SA, which now numbered 2 to 3 million men, was to be the nucleus of a great German revolutionary Army which would sweep nazism over Europe. As such it would supersede and engulf the regular Army.

In February 1934, Roehm presented a memorandum to Hitler's Cabinet (of which he was now a member) suggesting that the SA be made the foundation of a new "People's Army." The reaction on the part of the German Officers' Corps and of the General Staff to this interesting proposal was summed up by General von Brauchitsch at Nuremberg when he said: "Rearmament was too serious and difficult a business to permit the participation of peculators, drunkards, and homosexuals."

To complicate matters further, Hitler and the General Staff now received word that President von Hindenburg's days were numbered. The old Field Marshal was slowly dying on his estate at Neudeck in East Prussia. Hitler knew that the Army and certain conservative circles were prepared to proclaim a return to the Hohenzollern Monarchy upon the President's death; this he had to prevent at all costs, for of course he intended to assume the title of President himself.

On April 11, 1934, Hitler and the high Army commanders, as well as Admiral Raeder, took a brief cruise on the pocket battleship *Deutschland*. Hitler informed them that Hindenburg was dying and proposed that the Army support him as the old man's successor. In return he promised to suppress Ernst Roehm's ambitions, reduce the SA drastically, guarantee the Army and Navy their accustomed privileges in the German state, and drive for a tremendous expansion of German military power. After hasty consultations, the generals and admirals agreed to his terms. Events now moved rapidly to their bloody climax. During the next few weeks Hitler successfully convinced himself that his old crony Ernst Roehm was secretly plotting to kill him and seize power. Goering and Goebbels were given a free hand to prepare against this trumped-up threat, and the tension built steadily in Berlin as Hitler steeled himself for the showdown. His opportunity came on June 30, 1934. For on that day the chiefs of the SA, Roehm included, were holding a meeting at Wiessee, a small village near Munich. While Goering's police and Himmler's SS men started arresting SA leaders in Berlin, Hitler and a large party drove down to Munich in a long column of cars. They arrived shortly after dawn on June 30, to find Roehm and his aides still in bed. While Roehm's followers were dragged out of their beds and shot, Hitler personally confronted his oldest friend and supporter. After screaming hysterical accusations at the startled Roehm, Hitler ordered him arrested and transported to the Stadelheim Prison in Munich. There, again on Hitler's orders, a pistol was left in Roehm's cell. But the brawling ex-chief of the SA refused to use it. "If I am to be killed, let Adolf himself do it!" he cried. Whereupon two SS officers entered his cell and shot him to death.

And in Berlin, Goering and Goebbels had not been idle: 150 SA leaders were arrested, carried off to the Cadet School at Lichterfelde, and shot by SS firing squads. None of them knew why—many died shouting *"Heil Hitler!"* Karl Ernst, the Berlin SA leader who perhaps knew too much about the Reichstag fire, was shot along with them.

Nor were SA men the only victims of this "Blood Purge." For Hitler took the occasion to murder political opponents of all types as well as purely personal enemies. Thus, on the morning of June 30, a squad of SS men rang the doorbell of General Kurt von Schleicher's villa outside Berlin. When the general, who had belatedly opposed Hitler's seizure of power, answered the door, he was shot dead in his tracks. As his wife rushed to him she also was shot dead. Gregor Strasser, one of Hitler's most important followers, who had so brilliantly organized the Nazi party in Prussia and had then differed with Der Fuehrer, was murdered on Goering's personal orders in the Gestapo jail in Berlin. Franz von Papen, still nominally Vice-Chancellor of Germany, was merely arrested. But his personal secretary and various aides were shot by SS murder squads. Gustav von Kahr, who had "betrayed" Hitler during the Beer Hall *Putsch* and later testified against him at his trial, was dragged into a swamp near the Dachau Concentration Camp, where he had been imprisoned, and hacked to death with a pickax. Although exact figures have never been unearthed, it is estimated that the number of victims reached more than one thousand.

Most of the killing was over by July 1. On the following day President von Hindenburg roused himself from his torpor to thank Hitler for his "determined action and gallant personal intervention [!] which have nipped treason in the bud and rescued the German people from a great danger." Nor was the Army and its General Staff tardy in presenting their thanks to Der Fuehrer for "defending the state." Hitler himself, addressing the Reichstag on July 13, declared: "If anyone reproaches me and asks why I did not resort to the regular courts of justice, then all I can say is this: In this hour I was responsible for the fate of the German people. I became the supreme judge of the German nation. . . . Everyone must know for all future time that if he raises his hand to strike the state then certain death is his lot!" And when President von Hindenburg breathed his last on August 2, 1934, Hitler immediately proclaimed the abolition of the office of President and the assumption of supreme power in Germany by himself. To complete the *Deutschland* pact the German Officers' Corps and each and every individual in the German Army now stepped forward to swear allegience not to Germany, but to Adolf Hitler personally:

"I swear by God this sacred oath, that I will render unconditional obedience to Adolf Hitler, the Fuehrer of the German Reich and people, Supreme Commander of the Armed Forces, and will be ready as a brave soldier to risk my life at any time for this oath."

Thus the German Army and its Officers' Corps swore themselves into absolute fealty to the moral degeneracy and intellectual corruption of nazism. But they were by no means alone. For in a nationwide plebiscite (vote) on whether or not they approved Hitler's assumption of supreme power, on August 19, 1933, the German people voted 90 percent in favor of Der Fuehrer and his government of criminals and thugs. Hitler immediately proclaimed: "The German form of life is definitely determined for the next thousand years."

The life of a German was organized almost from the moment he was born—incidentally, the Nazi party hammered home the duty of every German girl to bear children for Der Fuehrer's Reich, in or out of wedlock —and that organization was directed and shaped by some of the most perverted minds ever to stain the pages of history. From the age of six until the age of ten a German boy served a sort of apprenticeship in the Hitler Youth. He was given a performance book in which every detail of his progress—especially his ideological progress—was noted. At the age of ten, after passing tests in athletics, outdoor subsistence, and the Nazi version of history (an incredible mishmash of nonsense and lies), he graduated into the Young People's section of the Hitler Youth. On entering he swore:

"In the presence of this blood banner, which represents our Fuehrer, I swear to devote all my energies and my strength to the savior of our country, Adolf Hitler. I am willing and ready to give up my life for him, so help me God."

At the age of fourteen the boy entered the Hitler Youth proper, and there he remained until he was eighteen, when he would enter either the Labor Service or the Army.

Head of the Hitler Youth, and responsible directly to Der Fuehrer, was Baldur von Schirach, a young man who had joined the Nazi party in 1925 at the age of eighteen. Von Schirach was not the most intelligent of men, to say the least. He followed the anti-Christian paganism of Alfred Rosenberg, the party "philosopher," and propagated the vile anti-Semitism of Julius Streicher. Any German parents who tried to keep their children out of von Schirach's hands could be sent to prison for many years.

The German schools and universities, which had once served as models to the world, were quickly nazified. On April 30, 1934, Bernhard Rust, a brawling Group Leader in the SA and a longtime follower of Hitler, was appointed Minister of Science, Education, and Popular Culture. Under his guidance German textbooks were quickly rewritten and the schools turned into Nazi propaganda machines. All teachers had to swear loyalty to Hitler and after 1938 had to have served in the SA, the Labor Service, or the Hitler

Youth. Children were taught "racial science" (*i.e.*, hatred and contempt for all non-Germans), Nazi history (*i.e.*, how the world conspired to deprive Germany of its place in the sun), and those mathematics and natural sciences best calculated to train young minds for military service.

The impact of nazism on education at the university level was disastrous. At the University of Berlin, for example, a loutish Stormtrooper, a veterinarian, was named Rector. He at once instituted twenty-five courses in "racial science" and eighty-six courses in veterinary medicine. World-famous professors, such as Albert Einstein, were fired because they were Jews. And subjects such as physics, chemistry, and mathematics were twisted and hammered into unrecognizable shapes in an attempt to make them prove Nazi theories. The cost of German higher education of such idiocy was profound. After six years of Nazi control German universities had lost more than half their students. And the competence of those who remained had fallen so low, even in such fields as engineering and chemistry, that the industries which relied on university graduates to direct their expansion programs publicly complained that both the German economy and the national war effort were being crippled by the low level of graduate scientists and engineers. Of greater interest to Americans was the fact that many of Germany's most brilliant and morally upright scientists fled from Hitler to find refuge in the United States. Besides making a profound contribution to American university life, these men were a great asset to the American war effort against Hitler. Albert Einstein, who finally settled at the Institute for Advanced Study at Princeton, had already given the world his theory of relativity, the foundation of modern physics. Humanity can be thankful that his ideas were dismissed in Germany as "Jewish physics," for it was upon his thought and with

the help of many German scientists in exile that the
United States was able to develop the atom bomb,
while Germany could not.

Hitler had stated, on November 6, 1933: "When an
opponent declares, 'I will not come over to your side,'
I calmly say, 'Your child belongs to us already. . . .
What are you? You will pass on. Your descendants,
however, now stand in the new camp. In a short time
they will know nothing else but this new community.' "
In raising up a generation of strong but mindless
young fanatics, Hitler was as good as his word. And
into what kind of community would a young Nazi
emerge?

If he was a peasant, he found himself enmeshed in
the security and slavery of a society which had returned to the Middle Ages. The Hereditary Farm Law,
which was proclaimed on September 29, 1933, reim-
posed semifeudal conditions on the German peasantry.
Thus, while the farmer was protected in his ownership
of the land, he was also bound to it like a serf. He
could not leave the land, nor could he stop working it,
nor could he dispose of it in any way except through
his death. Practically every action of his working day
was supervised by the government, as were the prices
he received for his produce and the prices he had to
pay for seed and equipment.

If our young Nazi entered the ranks of the working
class upon his graduation from the Hitler Youth, he
found himself a slave in all but name. The trade
unions had been abolished, of course, and with them
the right to strike, the right to bargain for higher
wages, and even the right to change jobs. Dr. Robert
Ley's National Labor Front decided all industrial questions regarding workers. In every factory the owners
were declared to be the "leaders," and the workers the
"followers." Factory owners became, in a sense, feudal
lords who, while they guaranteed the security of their

workers, expected long, hard work and blind obedience from them. Wages were kept as low as possible. In 1936 the average German industrial wage was $6.29 a week—lower than it had been before Hitler came to power—while German big business profits jumped 146 percent from 1933 to 1938. Nor was the German worker able to take home his miserable $6.29 per week; taxes and "voluntary" contributions to Nazi organizations took as much as 25 percent of it on the average. Beginning in 1935, every German worker was required to keep a "work book," which was a complete record of his employment, and in 1938 labor conscription was instituted. German workers were drafted to industries under rules which were as harsh as military discipline. Any worker who was absent too often, for example, could be sent to prison for many years.

Why did the mass of German workers, with their Socialist background, accept this daily tyranny? Largely because under Hitler unemployment was wiped out. Germany had over 6 million unemployed in 1933, but by 1936 there were less than a million, and thereafter there were labor shortages. Of course this was the result of a vast public works and rearmament program and of the drafting of millions of young people into the expanding German Army, but to the German worker, who remembered the bitter years of the depression, security evidently meant more than liberty. Besides that, Dr. Ley's National Labor Front organized very cheap recreational programs for German workers. Setting up an organization called "Strength through Joy," the Labor Front arranged mass vacations at the seaside and in the mountains and even foreign travel for its members. It also arranged one of the greatest swindles in history—the Volkswagen, or "People's car." Hitler, who was annoyed that there was only one car for every fifty Germans while in the United States there was one car for every five Americans, decreed that German industry should manufacture a car which would sell for only $395. But since German industry could by no means manufacture an automobile for such a low price, the Labor Front was ordered to build national factories to produce it. These factories were financed by payment in advance by German workers. When a German worker had paid up his $395, he was given a ticket with a number which would entitle him to a Volkswagen as soon as it could be produced. Unfortunately no Volkswagens were ever manufactured until after the Second World War, nor was any money ever refunded to the German workers.

German businessmen, while not directly enslaved as were German workers and German peasants, soon found that they were hopelessly entangled in government regulations, restrictions, and red tape. They were told what to produce, how to produce it, where to sell it and for how much, and practically every detail of their activities was rigorously controlled. The whole German economy, after 1934, was directed to the coming war with the purpose of making Germany immune to blockade. Under the financial wizardry of Hjalmar Schacht, German money was juggled in such a way that the financing of rearmament was largely hidden from the outside world, while, under government control, the giant Ruhr industries such as Krupps and I. G. Farben were harnessed to Hitler's "Guns before butter" program. The leaders of Germany's giant industrial enterprises profited greatly from German rearmament and from the strict Nazi control of labor. But for small businessmen life in Nazi Germany was complicated, to say the least.

And what of culture in Hitler's Germany? On the evening of May 10, 1933, a scene took place in Berlin which was symbolic of the Nazi attitude toward culture. On that night a torchlight parade of thousands of students marched through the city to the square in front of the University of Berlin. There they set fire to a pile of thousands of books. The books included not only the works of anti-Nazi or Jewish-German authors such as Thomas Mann, Lionel Feuchtwanger, Stefan Zweig, Erich Maria Remarque, and Albert Einstein— they also included the works of non-German writers from Jack London to André Gide, from H. G. Wells to Emile Zola. Goebbels, who watched the book burning with an approving eye, announced that the soul of the German people could once again express itself and that the flames of the burning books would illuminate a new era.

The new era in German culture was defined by absolute state control of books, newspapers, films, radio, art, music, and the theater. And, as German writers, artists, newspapermen, and dramatists either fled Hitler's regime or were destroyed by it, within a very short time German culture was reduced to a level of stupidity and outright boredom, which even the Nazis found wearisome. Thus, until 1939, Germans depended for truthful news on the broadcasts of foreign radio stations such as England's BBC, while even "Grade B" Hollywood films drew huge audiences who could not abide incompetent Nazi film-making. And when, in 1937, Hitler opened an exhibit of Nazi painting in Munich (he had personally selected the paintings, kicking holes in those he did not like), Germans stayed away in droves. Only in the field of music did German cultural standards remain relatively high. Although the works of such Jewish composers as Mendelssohn were forbidden, many of Germany's leading musicians such as Richard Strauss, Wilhelm Furtwaengler, and Walter Gieseking lent their fame and talent to the Nazi regime. But they were isolated phenomena on the vast, barren wasteland of German cultural life.

And as German culture was degraded, so too was

German Christianity brought under control and then perverted to Nazi ends. Hitler himself had been born a Catholic but had quickly forgotten, if he had ever learned, Christian doctrine. The Catholic Youth League was dissolved as part of Hitler's drive to regiment German youth, and Erich Klausener, a Catholic political leader, was murdered in the Blood Purge of June 30, 1934. In the following years thousands of Catholic priests and nuns were arrested and sent to concentration camps. By 1937 the Catholic Church leadership in Germany had suffered such persecution at Hitler's hands that Pope Pius XI issued an encyclical entitled *Mit Brennender Sorge* (With Burning Sorrow), in which he charged the Nazi government with lies, violence, hatred of Christian doctrine, and the planning of war and extermination.

The German Protestant churches fared no better under the Nazi regime. Most German Protestants (more than 45 million of them) were, of course, Lutherans and Reformed (Prussian Union). And in Luther's preaching of obedience to the state and to authority, many German Protestants saw a justification of their obedience to the detestable Nazi government. Nor did the Protestant clergy at first raise their voices to protest the bestiality of Hitler's doctrines. The Rev. Martin Niemoeller, for example, welcomed the Nazi victory. It was only after Hitler revealed in unmistakable fashion his intention of taking over the Protestant churches and of using them to preach a new form of paganism that Niemoeller and a handful of other Protestant leaders protested. Their fate was not unlike that of all others who objected to Nazi policies: they were arrested and jailed. Pastor Niemoeller was sent to a concentration camp. But before he was silenced, Martin Niemoeller preached one last sermon in his church at Dahlem. Foreseeing his own arrest, he said: "We have no more thought of using our own powers to escape the arm of the authorities than had the Apostles of old. No more are we ready to keep silent at man's behest when God commands us to speak. For it is, and must remain, the case that we must obey God rather than man."

As to what the Nazis intended to make of Christianity and churches of all denominations, that was made abundantly clear by a program outlined by Alfred Rosenberg, the boozy "philosopher" whom Hitler had appointed "Fuehrer's Delegate for the Entire Intellectual and Philosophical Education and Instruction for the National Socialist Party." In his outline for a National German Church, Rosenberg stated: "The National Church is determined to exterminate . . . the strange and foreign Christian faiths imported into Germany in the ill-omened year 800. . . . The National Church demands immediate cessation of the publishing and distribution of the Bible in Germany. . . . The National Church will clear away from its altars all crucifixes, Bibles, and pictures of saints . . . there must be nothing on the altars but *Mein Kampf* (to the German nation, and therefore to God, the most sacred book) and to the left of the altar a sword."

But of all the elements of German national life the greatest suffering was reserved for the Jews. Jews were the objects of Adolf Hitler's most insane hatred, and, although individual Germans tried to help individual German Jews during the Nazi period, the German people as a whole accepted the persecution and eventual extermination of the Jews with complete apathy.

On September 15, 1935, the so-called Nuremberg Laws were decreed against the Jews. Under these and later laws Jews were deprived of German citizenship (they were henceforth to be "subjects"), forbidden to marry non-Jews, forbidden to work in the civil service or any branch of the government, forbidden to practice professions such as law or medicine, excluded from journalism, radio, theater, the arts, farming, and teaching—in fact, forbidden to earn a living at any but the most menial jobs, and even these were hard to get. By 1936 at least one half of all German Jews were without work. Against Jews the SA and the SS, never known for their mercy in any case, showed no restraint. The murder of Jews, young or old, was a common occurrence in any German city or town, and one which was applauded by the government and ignored by the citizenry. As yet (until the start of World War II) Hitler had developed no program of complete annihilation of the Jews, but their life was made intolerable and what the future held for them was made clear. A little more than half of Germany's half million Jews were able to flee the country, usually stripped of all their belongings before they left. But for those who were unable to escape, the future held little hope.

And, in fact, by 1935 there was no hope for any German—no hope of overthrowing nazism. Those Germans dedicated and fearless enough to oppose Hitler were already dead or crowding the concentration camps that had sprung up throughout the country to house Der Fuehrer's enemies. For the vast majority of the German people the loss of liberty, the degradation of their lives, their own enslavement were to be compensated by the glories of revived German militarism and foreign conquest. Hypnotized by Hitler and prisoners of their own history, the German people followed Der Fuehrer blindly down a road that was to lead to overwhelming disaster—for themselves and for the world.

Five

THE ROAD TO WAR—I

WITH HITLER'S CONSOLIDATION OF POWER SECURE IN Germany, and with the vast German industry busily turning out munitions and armaments at full capacity, Der Fuehrer now felt himself obliged to carry out that program of German expansion which he had outlined in considerable detail in *Mein Kampf*. And the first steps in this program were to be the tearing up of the provisions of the Treaty of Versailles. Thus, on October 14, 1933, Germany withdrew from the League of Nations. Later, German rearmament (which, in spite of the secrecy with which the General Staff tried to surround it, was known to France and England) was to be made public, universal military service was to be instituted, and the Rhineland, that strategic industrial area of Germany west of the river Rhine which the Germans had been forbidden to fortify or occupy with troops, was to be militarized. But since Germany would remain relatively weak militarily for several years—until Hitler's huge war economy had a chance to rearm her—the Nazi government had to talk peace and proceed toward its goals cautiously.

How cautiously he would have to proceed was made

clear to Hitler on July 25, 1934. On that day Nazi thugs broke into the office of Chancellor Engelbert Dollfuss, the Fascist dictator of Austria, and shot him dead. Other Nazis seized the Vienna radio station and announced that Dollfuss had "resigned." The plot, directed from Germany, was intended to overthrow the Austrian government and bring about the *Anschluss* (annexation) of Austria to Germany. But within a few hours of Dollfuss' murder, Austrian government forces, led by Dr. Kurt von Schuschnigg, who now became Chancellor, put down the Nazi uprising in Vienna. And, more ominously, Mussolini, who had his own ambitions regarding Austria, mobilized four Italian Army divisions on the Italian-Austrian border. The English and French ambassadors in Berlin informed the German government that Austria must remain independent. Hitler quickly backed down. He did not yet have the necessary military force to confront a coalition of France, England, and Italy. He now proceeded to correct that situation.

On March 16, 1935, Hitler announced to the Reichstag and to the world that Germany was introducing universal military service and that the new German Army would expand to half a million men, that a German Air Force was already in being, and that the General Staff would once more resume its correct name and many of its former functions. This bold act was really a trial balloon. Many of the German generals were horrified. They feared an immediate French and English attack in response to this flouting of the Versailles Treaty. But Hitler was gambling that the internal political situation of the former Allies would prevent them from taking action—and he was right. France was torn by domestic political feuds, and England, still in the throes of depression and unemployment, wanted peace at almost any price. The victors of

World War I had no stomach for another war; they protested, but their words were empty.

Hitler now hastened to reassure the world that he was interested only in peace. On May 21, 1935, just a few days after announcing German rearmament, Der Fuehrer again addressed the Reichstag. "Germany needs peace and desires peace!" he proclaimed. Germany had solemnly recognized and guaranteed France her frontiers . . . Germany had concluded a non-aggression pact with Poland . . . Germany neither intended nor wished to interfere in the internal affairs of Austria. And the world believed him.

Hitler's next move came on March 7, 1936. At dawn on that day German troops, with bands blaring, marched across the Rhine bridges and reoccupied the demilitarized Rhineland. Although the move had been secretly planned for months, the General Staff was badly worried about it. For behind the blaring bands the German Army could muster only one division to reoccupy the Rhineland. If the French decided to fight over this final defiance of the Versailles Treaty, the German Army had made careful plans—to run as fast as it could back to the east side of the Rhine. But once again Hitler had correctly gauged his enemy's intentions and weaknesses. Later he was to admit: "The forty-eight hours after the march into the Rhineland were the most nerve-racking in my life. If the French had then marched into the Rhineland, we would have had to withdraw with our tail between our legs." But the French did not march. Unable to secure England's backing for any countermeasures, they had to content themselves with a formal protest.

Nor did Hitler fail to make his usual peace proposals. To the same hysterically cheering meeting of the Reichstag at which he had announced German reoccupation of the Rhineland, Der Fuehrer pledged that now, "more than ever," he would work for international understanding. He had no further territorial demands to make in Europe. "Germany," he swore, "will never break the peace." And the world believed him.

A few months later—on July 16, 1936—General Francisco Franco started a Fascist rebellion against the republican government of Spain. In need of planes, men, and other assistance in his drive to crush democracy in Spain, the general appealed to Italy and Germany for help. After talking the matter over with Goering and certain of the German commanders, Hitler decided to aid Franco. A German Air Force unit was organized—the Condor Legion—and dispatched to Spain as were various tank units and special advisers. But Hitler's purpose was not to assure Franco's victory—it was to ensure that the Spanish Civil War would go on as long as possible. For Mussolini had dispatched 70,000 men to fight for Franco as well as huge amounts of war matériel. And as long as the Italian dictator was involved in the Spanish struggle, England, which feared Fascist control of the Mediterranean Sea, and France, which feared the establishment of another Fascist enemy on her southern border, would remain at loggerheads with Italy. Thus Mussolini would be drawn more and more to rely on Germany as Italy's only friend.

Hitler had first met Benito Mussolini on June 14, 1934, at Venice. The newly risen German dictator in his shabby civilian clothes was made to feel inferior by Mussolini's bemedaled and gleaming military uniform and by the masses of well-drilled Italian Blackshirts who cheered Il Duce (The Leader) at his every word. In those days, in the dictatorship business, Hitler was definitely a junior partner to the well-established Mussolini. Now, with forces from both their countries fighting side by side in Spain, Der Fuehrer, on September 25, 1937, invited Mussolini to visit him in Germany. There the vain Italian dictator was flattered by Hitler and his followers, given ovations by the carefully rehearsed crowds of Nazis who greeted him wherever he went, and impressed by visits to German Army maneuvers, roaring Ruhr armament factories, and military parades. By the time he returned to Rome at the end of his four-day visit, Mussolini was convinced that the future was on Germany's side—and he determined to ally himself with it.

If the nervous generals of the German General Staff, who continued to be amazed at the success of Hitler's gambles, had any doubts as to where Hitler's policies were leading, these doubts were set to rest by Der Fuehrer himself at a meeting to which they were summoned at the Chancellery in Berlin on November 5, 1937. Present at this highly secret conference were Hitler and his military aide, Colonel Friedrich Hossbach; Field Marshal Werner von Blomberg, Commander in Chief of the German Armed Forces; General Werner von Fritsch, Commander in Chief of the Army; Admiral Erich Raeder, Commander in Chief of the Navy; Hermann Goering (now a general), Commander in Chief of the Air Force; and Baron Konstantin von Neurath, German Foreign Minister. In the space of four hours, during which Hitler did practically all the talking, he outlined his definite resolve and plans for a new war.

The aim of Germany policy, he advised his service chiefs, was to make secure and to preserve the racial community and to enlarge it. The Germans had the right to greater living space than other peoples. The only question remaining was when and where and under what circumstances Germany would strike. There were three sets of circumstances which would give Germany a good chance of success: First, on the completion of the German rearmament program in 1943. By that time Germany would be immeasurably more powerful than England and France combined.

On the other hand, those countries had started rearmament programs of their own, and if Germany waited beyond 1943, the scales would tip against her. Second, an opportunity to strike might come if France suffered such a severe internal crisis that she was unable to strike back. The domestic quarrels of French political parties were such that a civil war in that country could not be ruled out—and Germany must be prepared to take advantage of it if it came. Third, Germany's chance might come if France were to be tied down in a war with a third power. Here, Hitler had in mind Italy, with which France might become involved over the Spanish question. But, in any event, before Germany could take direct military action she would have to secure her flank by eliminating Austria and Czechoslovakia. Furthermore, Japan's help would have to be enlisted as a counterweight against possible Russian interference.

The German military commanders had had some hint of these plans in private discussions with Hitler, and indeed they had all been written down in *Mein Kampf*. But Hitler's words had a terrifying effect on most of those present. The German generals were horrified, not by the moral bankruptcy of Hitler's proposals but by their impracticality. Germany was unprepared for a general war—even by 1943 she would not be really ready. For Germany to embark on Hitler's program would lead to complete disaster, of that the generals were convinced. Yet Hitler now declared war to be his fixed purpose. Baron von Neurath was so disturbed that he suffered several heart attacks in the following weeks, while the Army commanders protested vehemently (with the backing of the General Staff) against what they considered a lunatic policy. But their objections led only to their removal. Baron von Neurath was replaced by Joachim von Ribbentrop as Foreign Minister. Von Ribbentrop, a former champagne salesman whose selling activities had brought him into contact with a few English and French aristocrats and whose bad manners and bullying behavior were combined with absolute adoration of Der Fuehrer, was the perfect errand boy for Hitler's deceitful foreign policy. Field Marshal von Blomberg and General von Fritsch were framed by the Nazis in distasteful personal scandals. Von Fritsch was replaced as Commander in Chief of the Army by General Walther von Brauchitsch. To replace von Blomberg as Commander in Chief of all the Armed Forces Hitler appointed—himself! From now on the German Army was to be Hitler's personal weapon of conquest.

Ever since Hitler's abortive attempt against Austrian independence by the murder of Chancellor Dollfuss in 1934, he had kept Austrian life in a turmoil. All through 1937 the Austrian Nazis, backed and financed by Berlin and led by a Viennese lawyer named Arthur Seyss-Inquart, stepped up their campaign of terror. Bombings were a daily occurrence, as were mass demonstrations that often erupted into violence. Dollfuss' successor as Austrian Chancellor, Dr. Kurt von Schuschnigg, was a man deeply devoted to the preservation of Austrian independence. When, therefore, the sly von Papen suggested that matters might be improved if Schuschnigg visited Hitler personally, the Austrian Chancellor was happy to agree.

When Schuschnigg arrived at Berchtesgaden, Hitler's mountaintop villa in the Bavarian Alps, to meet Der Fuehrer for what he supposed would be a friendly chat about the problems afflicting their two countries, he was surprised to find General Wilhelm Keitel (Hitler's personal Chief of Staff) and Generals Walther von Reichenau and Hugo Sperrle, the local Army and Air Force commanders, also in attendance. And if the presence of the military appeared ominous, Hitler's behavior was positively startling. When Schuschnigg opened their conversation with some graceful remarks about the fine view of the Alps Hitler enjoyed from his mountain perch, the Nazi dictator interrupted him rudely. "We did not gather here to speak of the weather!" Hitler barked. The "conversation" that followed this inauspicious beginning was both violent and one-sided.

"You have done everything to avoid a friendly policy!" Hitler exclaimed. "The whole history of Austria is just one uninterrupted act of high treason. . . . And I can tell you right now, Herr Schuschnigg, that I am absolutely determined to make an end of all this. The German Reich is one of the great powers, and nobody will raise his voice if it settles its border problems."

Stunned, Schuschnigg tried to stand up to Hitler's outbursts. But Der Fuehrer's rage seemed to feed on his own words.

". . . I am telling you once more that things cannot go on this way. I have a historic mission, and this mission I will fulfill because Providence has destined me to do so . . . who is not with me will be against me," Hitler ranted. "I have only to give an order, and in one single night all your ridiculous defense mechanisms will be blown to bits. You don't seriously believe you can stop me for half an hour, do you? . . . Don't think for one moment that anybody on earth is going to thwart my decision. Italy? I see eye to eye with Mussolini. . . . England? England will not lift one finger for Austria. . . . France? . . . Now it is too late for France."

Later the thunderstruck Austrian Chancellor was presented with a written ultimatum by Hitler. When he tried to protest, Hitler suddenly seemed to go out of his mind. Der Fuehrer raced to the doors, opened them, and bellowed: "General Keitel!" When Keitel came running and asked Hitler what his orders were, the Nazi dictator merely smiled and whispered: "There are no orders, I just wanted to have you here." But the bluff worked. Schuschnigg, imagining that this madman was calling upon General Keitel to order his army to march into Austria, quickly signed the agreement. And, as he expected, it was to prove Austria's death warrant.

For within the space of four weeks Austria would be so disrupted by Schuschnigg's agreement that it would be ripe for seizure.

In desperation Chancellor Schuschnigg decided to hold a nationwide plebiscite on March 13 in which the Austrian people would be asked whether they wanted to remain independent of Germany. There was no doubt in the Chancellor's mind that he would win such a vote.

Evidently there was none in Hitler's mind either. The Austrian vote had, at all costs, to be prevented. Therefore, on March 10, Hitler ordered the German Army to be prepared to invade Austria on March 12.

Orders went out at the same time to Seyss-Inquart and his Austrian Nazis to take over the government in Vienna. Once that had been accomplished, they were to send a telegram to Berlin requesting the presence of German troops to prevent disorder and riot.

By March 11, Vienna was a scene of chaos. Mobs of hysterical Nazis were rushing through the streets shrieking "Hang Schuschnigg! Heil Hitler!" The police looked on indifferently. Schuschnigg, still trying to maintain some sort of control on events, found himself drowned in confusion, disorder, and despair.

At about eight o'clock that night the haggard and defeated Austrian Chancellor broadcast to his people: "I take leave of the Austrian people with a German word of farewell, uttered from the depths of my heart: God protect Austria!"

On March 12, German troops poured over the Austrian frontier and Hitler accompanied them as far as

Linz. The people gave him a deliriously warm reception as he laid a wreath of flowers on the grave of his parents. On the following day the new Austrian government proclaimed: "Austria is a province of the German Reich." And on March 14 Hitler made his triumphal entry into Vienna. As he surveyed the city in which he'd been rejected as a vagrant so many years before, Hitler's mood was one of hysterical triumph— and vengeance.

Within a very few days Heinrich Himmler's SS troops and the dreaded Gestapo spread like some disease over the land. Political opponents—including Dr. Schuschnigg and his wife—were arrested and transported to German concentration camps by the thousands. And day after day thousands of Jewish men and women were made to scrub the gutters of Vienna while Nazi Stormtroopers stood over them and crowds gathered to jeer and taunt them. Thousands of others were jailed. Almost all were robbed of all their belongings. Later the Nazis set up an "Office for Jewish Emigration" run by Himmler's SS under the supervision of Reinhard Heydrich (who soon earned his nickname: "Hangman Heydrich") and Adolf Eichmann. By turning over to this office whatever small possessions they retained, Jews might be granted passports to leave Austria. Soon, however, the Office of Jewish Emigration was to devote itself to shipping Austrian Jews to extermination centers in the east.

And what of Britain and France, who years before had guaranteed Austrian independence? They confined themselves to formal protests. When Russia suggested a conference to consider joint action against further aggression, the Conservative government of Great Britain, headed now by Prime Minister Neville Chamberlain, icily turned down the idea.

On November 5, 1937, Hitler had first told his generals about his plans to wipe out Austria and Czechoslovakia in preparation for war. Now Austria had been eliminated and Czechoslovakia was next on Der Fuehrer's timetable. Plans for the invasion of the Central European democracy had been drawn up as early as June 24, 1937. The blow was to be "carried out with lightning speed," as Hitler said in order to convince the Western Allies that any intervention on their part would be too late in any event. And, as always, Hitler planned his military blow in conjunction with political warfare—a political warfare based on close study of the Czechoslovak internal political situation.

Hitler's first move toward the obliteration of Czechoslovakia was to stir up trouble among the German minority which inhabited the border regions known as the Sudetenland. Ever since Hitler had come to power in Germany, a Nazi party had grown in strength among the Sudeten Germans under the leadership of a gymnastics teacher named Konrad Henlein. Henlein, who was financed from Berlin, was instructed by Der Fuehrer to start making demands on the Czech government—demands which could not be met. As Henlein said after receiving Hitler's instructions: "We must always demand so much that we can never be satisfied." Hitler ordered his generals to prepare for war against the Czechs not later than October 1, 1938.

But if the German General Staff had been frightened by Hitler's gamble on Austria, they were absolutely appalled by his plans against Czechoslovakia. The Chief of the General Staff, General Ludwig Beck, was convinced that any attack on Czechoslovakia would mean war against England and France—and possibly Russia. And with Germany's Westwall as yet only partially completed, that would spell disaster. For to man the incomplete German fortifications facing France the German Army could muster at that time only 31 divisions of regular troops and 7 reserve divisions—of doubtful military quality. Against these the French could hurl over 100 divisions and simply walk to Berlin. Nor was it by any means certain that the Germans could beat the Czech Army even if the Czechs fought alone. For even by stripping the Westwall of its defenders, the German Army could muster in all only 55 divisions to attack the 45 better-trained Czech divisions through the heavily fortified Czech defense line. And if Russia honored her pact to come to Czechoslovakia's assistance along with France, then Germany's days were numbered. General Beck worked out a detailed memorandum of exactly what would happen to Germany if she were stupid enough to attack Czechoslovakia at this time and sent it to General Walther von Brauchitsch, Commander in Chief of the German Army. He wanted Brauchitsch to call a conference of all German commanding officers, read them the memorandum, and then lead them in refusing to obey Hitler's orders, which could end only in disaster. A secret meeting at which all German Army and Corps commanders were present was called on August 4. General Beck read his own memorandum because General Brauchitsch was too frightened to do so. And, although the assembled officers took no immediate action (Beck had hoped they would all resign at once), they agreed with the General Staff that something had to be done. On August 18, General Beck resigned as Chief of the General Staff although none of the other generals had the courage to join him in his defiance.

To replace General Beck, Hitler now appointed General Franz Halder as Chief of the General Staff. But Halder agreed completely with Beck about the proposed attack on Czechoslovakia. Generals Halder and Beck, with the support of several other important generals, former diplomats, ex-trade-union leaders, and such key personalities as Admiral Wilhelm Canaris, Chief of German Intelligence and Counterespionage, and Count Wolf von Helldorf, Chief of the Berlin Police, now established a conspiracy to stop Hitler. Their plan was relatively simple. On the day that Hitler ordered the Germany Army to attack Czechoslovakia, the conspirators would arrest him and bring him before one of his own "People's Courts" on charges of leading Germany to disaster. Generals in command of forces around Berlin would seal off the capital against any attempt by the SS to interfere. Within Berlin other forces, aided by the Berlin police, would seize control of the government buildings and bring the Nazi regime to an end. Of course the whole basis of this plan was the conviction that England and France would fight to protect Czechoslovakia. With that certain, Beck and Halder were sure that the Army would support them and that once the German people understood where Hitler's madness was leading them, they too would support the conspirators. Plans were made for the arrest of such as Goering, Goebbels, and Himmler at the same time. With all the precise and scientific methods of General Staff work, the generals planned a swift surprise blow which would bring nazism to an end in Germany.

If many members of the conspiracy, such as the ex-trade-union leaders and diplomats, were opposed to Hitler on political and moral grounds, most of the conspiring generals were opposed simply because they knew that Germany could not win a general war. Among them only General Beck seems to have based his decision on a general hatred of the Hitler regime. Therefore, the essence of the plan's success lay precisely in a certain German defeat. If by any chance the Western Allies should not fight or if Hitler should gain the conquest of Czechoslovakia without endangering the continued existence of the German Army and nation, then the conspirators did not feel they could act with any hope of success. To make certain that England and France would stand up to Hitler, General

Beck and his coplotters sent several messengers to London over the next few months. These men warned the Chamberlain government as vividly as they knew how that Hitler was planning war and that he would strike at Czechoslovakia on October 1, 1938. They also told the English of their plan to do away with Der Fuehrer and asked only that England and France maintain a strong and belligerent front against him.

As the tense summer of 1938, which had seen widespread rioting in the Sudetenland and a huge campaign of lies and hatred directed against Czechoslovakia by Dr. Goebbels' efficient propaganda machine, drew to its close, Chamberlain sent a telegram to Hitler in which he proposed to meet the Nazi dictator "with a view to trying to find a peaceful solution." Der Fuehrer was stunned by this message. He had his heart set on war and now this bungling Englishman might disrupt his plans. On the other hand, he was flattered that the Prime Minister of the mighty British Empire was coming to see him, hat in hand, to beg for peace. He received Chamberlain on September 15, 1938, in the very room in which he had bullied and browbeaten Chancellor Schuschnigg six months before, in his private villa at Berchtesgaden.

Hitler began the conversation with a long harangue about how much he had done for peace, how brutally the Sudeten Germans were "persecuted" by the evil Czechs, and how determined he was that the Sudetenland would have to be returned to Germany "one way or the other."

In reply to Hitler's demands the British Prime Minister said that, while he personally agreed that the Sudetenland might be detached from Czechoslovakia, he had to get the approval of his government in London for such a step. He made Hitler promise not to take any military action until he had had a chance to consult his government and return to Germany on September 22. Since Hitler did not plan to attack before October 1 anyway, he was happy to make the promise.

While Chamberlain rallied support for his policy of appeasement among his own Cabinet and the French government the Germans went ahead with their plans for the destruction of Czechoslovakia. Hungary and Poland were approached with the suggestion that they jump in on the game and grab certain Czech territories on their borders. The Fascist Hungarian government of Admiral Miklós Horthy was only too pleased to be invited to share in the spoils, while the Polish government of Marshal Edward Smigly-Rydz, a reactionary regime headed by the Polish Army, also determined to join the prospective rape of Czechoslovakia.

But in order for England and France to give in to Hitler's demands—a policy they had long since decided upon—they had to persuade the Czech government to agree. On September 19, 1938, the British and French ambassadors in Prague advised that all Czech territories in which more than 50 percent of the population was German be turned over to Germany. Abandoned by its supposed friends, and allies, the Czech government caved in. It agreed to accept the Anglo-French terms.

Chamberlain, overjoyed that he could now bring Der Fuehrer all that had been asked, hurried off to Godesberg in Germany on September 22 to meet Hitler once again. Unknown to the British Prime Minister, the Nazi dictator had worked himself up into such a fury against the Czechs in the past few days that he had actually, on more than one occasion, hurled himself to the floor and chewed on the carpet.

When Chamberlain informed Hitler that he could now have the Sudetenland by peaceful agreement, Der Fuehrer was astonished. But he managed to control his surprise. "Do I understand that the British, French, and Czech governments have agreed to the transfer of the Sudetenland from Czechoslovakia to Germany?"

he asked. Chamberlain smiled assent. "I'm terribly sorry," Hitler declared, "but . . . the plan is no longer of any use." Like any common blackmailer, Hitler was raising his price as soon as it was met. Chamberlain was stunned. Hitler told him that only a *military occupation* by the German Army immediately would be considered—and handed him a map showing large areas of Czechoslovakia to be occupied. Furthermore, the Nazi dictator demanded that his terms be met not later than October 1. Chamberlain replied that Czechoslovakia would certainly not accept those terms (which included the expulsion of all Czechs from the Sudeten areas and the seizure of all their property) and that he doubted if the British government would accept them. But Hitler remained adamant. His only concession was to assure the British Prime Minister that after "solving" the Sudeten problem, he would make no further territorial demands in Europe—a statement which Chamberlain, incredible though it seems, believed.

Once again Chamberlain hurried back to England to gain support for further appeasement of Hitler. But, in the face of what was little more than an ultimatum from Hitler, the Western Allies also began to make ready their defenses. The French Army mobilized 100 divisions and began sending them to the German frontier. The English Fleet was placed on alert and a state of emergency proclaimed. The Czech Army of one million men also was mobilized.

Besides these threatening events, Hitler was now disturbed by appeals from the King of Sweden and from President Franklin D. Roosevelt of the United States to preserve the peace of the world. And when, in an attempt to whip up German enthusiasm for war, Der Fuehrer ordered a German division to parade through Berlin, the citizens ignored the parade, leaving no doubt that they did not welcome a new world war.

Hitler, perhaps slightly disheartened by these ill omens, and convinced that he could get Chamberlain to hand him what he wanted on a silver platter, now wrote a letter to the British Prime Minister in which he explained that his demands would not really destroy Czechoslovakia, and that once he had taken the Sudetenland, he would join England and France in guaranteeing the rest of Czechoslovakia against any further aggression. The letter was, of course, one long lie—nor did Hitler retreat from his October 1 deadline. But it worked. Neville Chamberlain clutched at it like a drowning man clutching at a log. Immediately he sent a telegram to Mussolini begging him to intercede with Der Fuehrer. The Italian dictator at once contacted Berlin and asked Hitler if he would be interested in a summit conference with England and France. Hitler, sure now that he could gain all his demands, agreed.

And so the great powers came to Munich—a city whose name was to stand ever after as a symbol of cowardice and betrayal. Not all the great powers came. Russia, whose Red Army was ready to guarantee Czech independence if the Allies agreed, was not invited. Neither was the victim, Czechoslovakia. But Prime Minister Chamberlain, the French Premier, Edouard Daladier, and the Italian dictator, Benito Mussolini, met with Hitler on September 29, 1938, to sacrifice the life of a cultured, liberty-loving democracy on the altar of appeasement of a madman's greed. The conference accomplished its task quickly. Mussolini said he had brought along a set of written proposals which would help speed the discussions. They were, in fact, almost exactly the demands Hitler had made in his last ultimatum. The proposals had been written by the German Foreign Office and supplied to Mussolini just before the conference. Chamberlain and Daladier accepted them at once.

Shortly after midnight, in the early hours of September 30, 1938, Chamberlain, Daladier, Mussolini, and Hitler affixed their signatures to the Munich Agreement. By its terms the German Army was to begin its march into Czechoslovakia's Sudetenland on October 1—the very date Hitler had set months before and from which he never deviated. Later that same day the Czech government in Prague, now deserted by its allies, gave in to the German demands.

Chamberlain returned to London in triumph. In his hand he carried a signed declaration by Hitler that he would continue to work for "the peace of Europe." "My good friends," Chamberlain told the crowds outside No. 10 Downing Street, ". . . there has come back from Germany to Downing Street peace with honor. I believe it is peace in our time." The crowds cheered. Later in Parliament, when Winston Churchill arose to say, "We have sustained a total, unmitigated defeat," he was shouted down.

And what of the German generals who had been conspiring to arrest Hitler when he ordered the German Army to march into Czechoslovakia? They had always counted on English and French refusal of Hitler's demands. But now, incredibly, the Allies had given Hitler everything he demanded. On the very day that Chamberlain and Daladier arrived in Munich, preliminary orders had gone out to Army units to commence operations according to the conspirators' plans. Now these orders were hastily rescinded. How could the Army strike down the Nazi dictator after he had won such an overwhelming and bloodless victory? The people would never support them—Hitler was at the very peak of his popularity in Germany. General Franz Halder is said to have lost control of himself when the news of Munich reached him. The Chief of the General Staff cried out, "What can we do? He succeeds in everything he does!"

Six

THE ROAD TO WAR-2

IF NEVILLE CHAMBERLAIN THOUGHT HE HAD RETURNED to England with "peace in our time," his illusions were quickly to be shattered. For Hitler had said, months before, that he was determined to *destroy* Czechoslovakia, not merely to amputate it. On October 5, 1938, at Hitler's insistence (and in fear for his life from Nazi assassins) Czech President Eduard Benes resigned and fled his country to find refuge in England. A few days later Poland and Hungary accepted Hitler's standing invitation and swooped down like vultures on the now helpless Czechs to seize large territories of the republic. And if this was not sufficient to clarify Hitler's real aims, the Nazi dictator forced the Czechs to install a pro-German government. The new President of Czechoslovakia was to be Dr. Emil Hácha, a weak and confused old man.

Chamberlain's government may have been misled by Hitler's constant harping on how he "wanted no Czechs" within German borders. On many occasions Der Fuehrer had insisted that to assimilate conquered non-Aryan races into the German Reich would be to weaken the "purity" of the German race. This had also been a heavily labored point in *Mein Kampf*. But if this was the case, the British Prime Minister should have read further along in Hitler's book. There he would have found detailed expression of that ancient German policy: conquest and enslavement of the east. Germany's "living space" was to be carved out of Czech, Polish, and Russian territory. On October 21, Hitler instructed his generals: "The future tasks for the armed forces [are] . . . the liquidation of the remainder of Czechoslovakia." In spite of Hitler's sworn promise to Chamberlain to respect and even guarantee the new frontiers of Czechoslovakia, the autumn of 1938 was full of evil omens of Der Fuehrer's true intentions.

An even more sinister omen of future German policy was revealed during the week of November 10–17, 1938, a week later referred to as the "Week of the Broken Glass." On November 7 a 17-year-old German Jewish boy named Herschel Grynszpan, whose father had been shipped to Poland in a boxcar from Germany along with ten thousand other Jews, shot and killed the third secretary of the German Embassy, Ernst vom Rath, in Paris. Hitler's fury was uncontrollable. On the night of November 9, Goebbels issued orders to the SS and to the police that a "spontaneous" demonstration against the Jews throughout Germany was to be organized. Jewish homes and synagogues were to be burned down—but care was to be taken that the fires did not spread to German property. Jews—especially rich Jews —were to be arrested, robbed, and shipped to concentration camps.

A night of pure horror followed these instructions. Synagogues and Jewish homes and shops throughout Germany went up in flames. Jewish men, women, and children who tried to escape the flames were shot down in the street by the waiting SS troopers and police. Bloodthirsty gangs of Nazi roughnecks broke into thousands of Jewish homes, where they plundered, raped, and killed at will. Over 200 synagogues were destroyed by fire, and more than 20,000 Jews were arrested. The number of killed, though never officially revealed, was believed to have reached over one thousand. There were no recorded instances of German citizens trying to help their neighbors.

Also clear, as 1938 gave way to the fateful year 1939, were Hitler's intentions toward the remainder of Czechoslovakia. As early as October 19 of the previous year Hitler had decided to foment civil strife in what remained of the republic and then use that as an excuse to march in German troops. Thus the Slovaks were encouraged (and even forced) to start agitating for a separate state of Slovakia independent of the Czechs. Hitler knew that if the Czech government accepted Slovak demands, it would mean the end of Czechoslovakia. If, on the other hand, they clamped down on the Slovakian troublemakers, it would give him an excuse to send in German troops to "preserve order." The intrigues, riots, threats, and uproar caused by the German-inspired Slovakian independence movement proved too much for President Hácha's Czech government. On March 14, 1939, the independent state of Slovakia was proclaimed —under German "protection." Faced with the disintegration of his country, the bewildered and aged President Hácha made a fatal mistake—he asked for a personal meeting with Hitler.

The formal arrangements were perfect. As President Hácha's train arrived at the Anhalt Station in Berlin on March 14, 1939, a German military guard of honor snapped to attention. He and Foreign Minister František Chvalkovsky were greeted by no less a dignitary than Joachim von Ribbentrop, the German Foreign Minister, who presented him with a bouquet of flowers for his daughter, who had also accompanied the aged President on his journey. He was given a luxurious suite in Berlin's famous Adlon Hotel and, when Hácha and Chvalkovsky finally arrived for discussions at the

German Foreign Ministry on the Wilhelmstrasse, an SS honor guard saluted them. Awaiting them were Hitler, Goering, Ribbentrop, General Keitel—and Dr. Theodor Morell, a mindless quack who was Hitler's personal physician.

President Hácha spoke first. Perhaps because he was so old, perhaps because he hoped to save his people from the final calamity, perhaps because he was intrinsically a weak man, the Czech President groveled before Hitler. He disclaimed all responsibility for the previous Czech government of Eduard Benes, proclaimed his adoration of Der Fuehrer, even wondered whether Czechoslovakia had the right to exist as a sovereign nation. But if Hitler had been angered by outbursts of anti-German feeling among the Czechs, he, President Hácha, could assure Der Fuehrer that he was doing everything in his power to suppress them.

Hitler listened to this recital in stony silence. When it was over, the storm broke. In his usual manner the Nazi dictator began by reciting all the alleged "wrongs" that Czechoslovakia had committed against Germany and Germans since the day of its foundation. Working himself up into one of his hysterical rages, Hitler finally screamed that his patience had ended. On March 12 he had already given the order for German troops to invade Czechoslovakia and bring that perfidious nation's existence to an end. The armies would march tomorrow, at 6 A.M. There were only two possibilities. Either the Czechs would offer resistance, in which case the German troops would crush the Czech people brutally, or President Hácha would sign a document of surrender immediately and order his people to receive the German Army peacefully, in which case the Czech people might be spared the worst. It was up to President Hácha to decide. And only a few hours remained before the Germans marched.

According to an eyewitness, President Hácha and

Foreign Minister Chvalkovsky "sat as though turned to stone. Only their eyes showed that they were still alive."

Hitler now withdrew and left the Czechs to the attentions of Goering and Ribbentrop. When Hácha and Chvalkovsky protested against the outrage being committed against their country, swearing that they would never sign the surrender documents, the fat Nazi Air Force Commander and slippery Foreign Minister shouted them down. They followed Hácha and Chvalkovsky around and around the table on which the surrender documents were lying, pushing the papers at them, forcing pens on them, screaming that if they did not sign, Prague would be destroyed by hundreds of Nazi bombers within a few hours. President Hácha fainted.

Goering instantly called for Dr. Morell (whose presence at the meeting was thus explained) to give President Hácha an injection. Somewhat revived, Hácha had just strength enough to telephone his government in Prague, advising surrender, and to stumble back to the table and sign the fatal documents. It was, as the old man realized, the death warrant for his country.

As Hitler had told Hácha, at 6 A.M. on that very morning of March 15, 1939, German troops poured over the borders of what remained of Czechoslovakia. The little republic was proclaimed a "protectorate" of Germany, and all power over its people now passed into the hands of German administrators—and of Himmler's SS and Gestapo. The usual Nazi campaigns of barbarism and savagery were unleashed against the helpless Czech people. And on March 16, the two-day life of independent Slovakia came to an end when German troops entered it. Hitler had no further use for the Slovakian fiction.

The brutal German annexation of Czechoslovakia brought at least one benefit to the world. Neville Chamberlain, with the newspapers and Parliament of England reacting in outrage to Hitler's latest treachery, suddenly saw the light.

On March 31, just two weeks after Hitler entered Prague, Chamberlain publicly guaranteed Poland protection against Nazi aggression. The guarantee (to which France adhered) was made into a treaty shortly afterward, and it was one Allied promise that would be kept.

Even before the final liquidation of Czechoslovakia the German campaign against Poland had commenced. At first it was limited to diplomatic pressure. When Poland's Foreign Minister, Colonel Józef Beck, visited Hitler at Berchtesgaden on January 5, 1939, he was informed that Germany wanted the port city of Danzig returned to the Reich. Danzig, an old German city on the shores of the Baltic Sea, had been declared a "Free City" under the terms of the Versailles Treaty. Its administration was in the hands of the League of Nations. It was surrounded by Polish territory—a narrow strip of land called the Polish Corridor, which provided Poland with access to the sea and split East Prussia from Germany. Besides the return of Danzig, Hitler wanted permission to build a superhighway and a double-track railroad across the corridor. In return he offered to guarantee Poland's German boundaries for twenty years. Colonel Beck was somewhat dismayed by these suggestions. But his dismay was to turn to deep distrust and finally to fear over the following months as German demands were made more and more insistently.

On April 3, Hitler issued a top secret directive to his armed forces to prepare for the invasion and conquest of Poland. The attack, under the code name of "Operation White," was to be made from newly conquered Czechoslovakia as well as from East Prussia and Germany. The tentative date of September 1, 1939, was set for commencing active operations. The old pattern of Nazi riot and disorder in Danzig would be used as a pretext for grabbing the Free City, while some more specific "provocation" would be thought out to justify the German assault on Poland itself. Meantime, the Nazi propaganda machine went into high gear, feeding the world, and especially the German population, wild stories of alleged Polish brutality against defenseless Germans in Poland.

It was in April, too, that Mussolini finally made up his mind to ally himself and his country to the fortunes of Nazi Germany. Previously, while generally supporting Hitler at every opportunity, the Italian dictator had been careful not to bind the country formally to German policy. But on May 22, 1939, Count Galeazzo Ciano, Mussolini's son-in-law and Italian Foreign Minister, signed the so-called "Pact of Steel" with Germany in the Chancellery in Berlin. By its terms Italy and Germany promised to come to the assistance of each other if either of them should go to war. As a finishing touch to the signing ceremonies Ciano presented German Foreign Minister von Ribbentrop with a gaudy Italian decoration known as the Collar of the Annunziata. At this Hermann Goering, who decorated his paunch with any medals he could find, burst into tears. The collar really should have gone to him, he protested, as he had really been the chief promoter of the treaty. Ciano promised to try to get him one.

On May 23, 1939, Hitler finally issued a comprehensive directive to his military commanders—not simply for war against Poland but for war against England and France too, although Der Fuehrer still had some slight hopes that they might betray Poland as they had betrayed Czechoslovakia. Forecasting with amazing accuracy the course the war would take, he declared: "The aim must be to deal the enemy a smashing or a finally decisive blow right at the start. Considerations of right or wrong, or of treaties, do not enter into the matter. . . . If we succeed in occupying and securing Holland and Belgium, as well as defeating France, the basis for a successful war against England has been created. The Luftwaffe can then closely blockade England . . . and the fleet undertake the wider blockade with submarines."

On the last day of May the Russian Foreign Minister, Vyacheslav Molotov (Maxim Litvinov had been dismissed because of the apparent failure of his policy of trying to cooperate with the Western Allies), made an ominous speech in Moscow. It was time, he declared, for the Western powers to decide whether they really wanted to oppose Hitler or not. The Soviet Union was gaining the impression that England and France hoped to force Russia alone into a war with Germany. But if the Allies were serious about an anti-Nazi agreement, then they should at once send high-ranking representatives to Moscow to start talks. He hinted that, if this was not done, some arrangement might be made between Russia and Germany. Although Prime Minister Chamberlain still deeply distrusted Russian intentions, held an ingrained dislike of Communist principles, and clung to a suspicion that the Red Army would be an ineffective ally in any case, he bowed to the urgings of other members of his Cabinet and of Parliament and agreed to send a British-French military mission to Moscow. Hitler, who had paid close attention to the shifts in Soviet foreign policy, decided at the same time that there might be some possibility of an agreement between Germany and Russia. From now on Britain and Germany would be competing for Russian favor.

To the people of Western Europe it seemed incredible that Nazi Germany and Communist Russia could ever come to any sort of understanding. For, next to the Jews, Hitler hated Communists above all. Every

one of Der Fuehrer's speeches had been liberally sprin-
kled with insults for the Soviet Union and its rulers.
Besides that, the German drive to conquer the east, the
Drang nach Osten, had been a part of German policy
since the days of Charlemagne. On the part of Russia
and Communist parties throughout the world, this
hatred was returned with interest. Russian policy for
years had been an attempt to form an alliance with
other nations for the sole purpose of crushing nazism
and fascism. Russia had joined the League of Nations
only for that reason and Germany had left the League
protesting that Russia wanted to turn it into anti-Nazi
ends. But the Western Allies overlooked a few factors
in this equation. First of all, whatever the ideological
differences between nazism and communism, the German General Staff had always tried to pursue a pro-
Russian policy. Only with the cooperation of Russia,
they knew, could Germany avoid that most dreadful of
possibilities—a two-front war. And only with Russian
agreement could Poland be once again conquered and
divided to provide Germany land and slaves. Russian-
German cooperation at the expense of the Poles had
an ancient, if dishonorable history. And, it will be recalled, Russian cooperation helped make possible the
rebirth of the German Army in the years immediately
following World War I. Hitler, to the disgust of his
generals, had done away with that cooperation and
based his policy on open hatred of the Soviet Union. It
was this oft-expressed hatred which led many Western
politicians to imagine that they could appease Hitler in
such a way that the German fury would be directed
east. But Hitler understood the dangers of a two-front
war almost as well as his General Staff. And in *Mein
Kampf* he had clearly stated that German policy must
be to defeat the West first in order to be free to conquer the East. In spite of his harsh words for Russia,
this was the policy he now followed.

Meanwhile, German provocations in the Free City of Danzig had mounted. The local Nazis, under Berlin's direction, began interfering with Polish officials in the performance of their duty. Polish customs inspectors were particularly subject to personal threats—largely because German officers and weapons were being smuggled past them into Danzig. Poland retaliated by arming her customs inspectors. When Hitler learned of this, he was stung to fury. Angry notes poured into Warsaw from the German government. But the Poles replied that "they would continue to react as hitherto to any attempt by the authorities of the Free City to impair rights and interests which Poland enjoys in Danzig, and that they will regard any intervention by the Reich Government . . . as an act of aggression." No one had spoken to Hitler like this since he came to power—his reaction was to step up preparations for the invasion of Poland on September 1, according to his plan.

By August 5, with tension mounting throughout Europe, Chamberlain finally sent a team of military negotiators to Russia. Chamberlain's policy was still founded on mistrust of the Russians more than on fear of the Germans. This was shown by the fact that his negotiators were under instructions to proceed as slowly as possible in their talks with the Russians. It was also shown by the low level of Army and Navy brass who were sent. Whereas the Russians intended to send the top commanders of their Army, Air Force, and Navy to the conference table, the Western Allies were to be represented by comparatively junior officers. Besides that, the Russians quickly learned that the Allied team did not intend to impart any secret military information to them and, in fact, that they had even "forgotten" their own credentials!

The entire course of the Allied-Russian negotiations in Moscow, which dragged on until August 23, only confirmed Stalin's suspicions that the West did not seriously seek an anti-Hitler alliance with the Soviet Union.

By that time, in any case, it was too late. Hitler had acted, and as usual he had acted decisively and speedily. His final decision to reach an agreement with Russia had been taken during the last week of July and the first week of August. He now pressed negotiations forward with incredible speed. Of course, he had already set September 1 as the invasion date for Poland, and therefore desperately needed a pact with the Soviet Union in a matter of days. The Nazi ambassador to Moscow, Count Fritz von der Schulenberg, pressed forward his secret talks with the Russian Foreign Minister Molotov during the first two weeks of August. Telegrams from Berlin constantly urged speed upon him. He was instructed to agree to each and every Russian demand. It was clear that Hitler wanted an agreement with Russia at almost any price—and he wanted it immediately.

On August 23, 1939, German Foreign Minister Joachim von Ribbentrop, who had arrived with a large party by air the day before, signed a Nazi-Soviet Non-aggression Pact in Moscow. By the public terms of the agreement Russia and Germany promised not to attack each other and to maintain an attitude of benevolent neutrality toward each other if either became engaged in war with any other nations. There were secret agreements attached to the treaty which provided that Russia should have a free hand in "solving" the problems of the former Russian border regions which had been lost by the Soviet Union at the end of World War I. Thus Hitler agreed to allow Russia to seize the countries of Latvia, Lithuania, and Estonia, which had gained their freedom in 1919, to force Romania to return to Russia the province of Bessarabia, which she had taken in 1919, and—most vital of all—that conquered Poland would be divided with Russia, Soviet forces occupying those areas in eastern Poland inhabited primarily by Russians which Poland had conquered from the young Soviet state in 1920.

The news of the signing of the Nazi-Soviet Non-aggression Pact came as a stunning blow to the West. It even came as a stunning blow to Communist parties throughout the world. By assuring that Germany would not have to fight a two-front war, it made Nazi aggression against Poland and the West all but certain. The Soviet dictator's blindness was to cost the Allies dearly now—and Russia later.

During the feverish summer of 1939, Mussolini, in spite of the "Pact of Steel," grew more and more afraid of the coming war. He had already told Hitler that Italy would not be ready for war before 1943. Until then the Italian lack of raw materials and of armament would cripple any war effort Italy undertook. And if Hitler went to war against England and France, Mussolini feared that the Western Allies would fall with all their strength upon Italy if she should ally herself with Germany.

In an attempt to find out what was on Hitler's mind, Mussolini dispatched Foreign Minister Ciano to Germany for talks with Hitler and Ribbentrop on August 11. There the cunning Ciano was to receive the shock of his life.

Over dinner at an inn near Salzburg, on August 11, the Italian Foreign Minister asked: "Well, Ribbentrop, what do you want? The [Polish] Corridor or Danzig?"

"Not that any more," Ribbentrop replied, staring at Ciano with his icy-blue, fanatical eyes. "We want war!"

Ciano returned to Rome to write in his diary: "I return to Rome completely disgusted with the Germans, with their leader, with their way of doing things."

The German "way of doing things" was to be illustrated by a plan of which Ciano had not the faintest idea. Hitler had always made a point of fabricating some sort of excuse for aggression against his neighbors. And Poland was to be no exception; a border "incident" was to be staged by the SS and the Gestapo. Given the code name "Operation Himmler," and led by a tough SS agent named Alfred Naujocks, the plan was to dress up a few SS men in Polish Army uniforms and have them attack the German radio station at Gleiwitz on the Polish border. The raid was to be a real one, with live ammunition and explosives. To lend it an aspect of bloody realism, several concentration camp inmates were to be killed and left, dressed in Polish Army uniforms, near the radio transmitter. Then the German press and radio would trumpet this "Polish attack on German territory" to the world and to the German people—and Hitler's armies would have an excuse to march. That such a crude plan would be obvious to any informed observer did not matter; it was primarily intended to whip up war enthusiasm among the German people, and they were hardly well-informed after six years of Dr. Goebbels' stranglehold on the truth.

Hitler felt, in any event, that the German Army was ready for action. Already the German economy had been put on a war footing under the direction of Hermann Goering. The giant Ruhr industries were turning out arms at a tremendous rate. Military training had produced 50 divisions and would soon turn out hundreds more. The German Army boasted 9 armored divisions—deadly formations such as no other country in the world then possessed—and would soon have many more. The German Air Force of 21 squadrons (260,000 men) was far and away larger and more efficient than the Air Forces of England, France, and Russia combined. The German Navy, although comparatively weak as opposed to the British, had two huge and modern battleships, the *Bismarck* and the *Tirpitz*, several pocket battleships and, more importantly, 50 submarines—and would soon have many more undersea boats. The Westwall fortifications, although still incomplete, were now strong enough to deter any French attack from the west. And, of course, most important of all, Hitler now knew that Russia would not intervene against him. Therefore, when he called his top military commanders together on August 22, 1939, for a final general conference before the war, Der Fuehrer was in a swaggering mood. As usual at these conferences, Hitler did all the talking. That he must have been extremely boring to the assembled generals and admirals goes without saying. But by this time the military was used to groveling before him. In all the records of military conferences held by Hitler before the war, there are no more than one or two occasions on which anyone present dared to interrupt or even to question him.

Hitler opened his monolog by revealing some of the considerations which had prompted him to make war immediately. The first of these was the fact of his own existence and that of Mussolini. Two such geniuses, two such able leaders of their nations, two such talented men would probably not appear again for hundreds of years in German and Italian history. Nor was there any great personality to be found in the Allied camp—certainly no one to match himself.

After the generals had swallowed this, Hitler rambled on about the great military weakness and moral decay of England and France. Every day that he waited to launch his war, the Allies were rearming while their courage was ebbing. It was still highly improbable that they would fight. But if they did—better now than later. As for Germany, she had nothing to lose in case of war; she could only gain. Nor would it be a long war. Neither England nor France could stand a long war. And by his own resolution and genius Hitler had assured Russian neutrality. Never again would the General Staff have to plan on the nightmare of a two-front war. That was a mistake that the Emperor had made, which he would not repeat. All in all, the prospects for quick victory were excellent. The only thing he feared was that Chamberlain or some other dirty dog would make new peace proposals.

To close his hours-long speech, Hitler gave the gathered generals a rousing climax. "Close your hearts to pity!" Der Fuehrer roared. "Act brutally! Eighty million people must obtain what is their right! The stronger man is right! Be harsh and remorseless! Be steeled against all signs of compassion!"

Hermann Goering led the applause.

It was too late now for peace. General Halder, Chief of the General Staff, had already received his instructions. German armies were mobilizing in East Prussia, Czechoslovakia, and Pomerania for the descent on Poland. Other German troops were taking up their stations in the Westwall. The German Navy had sailed for Atlantic waters, and the German Air Force had been put on the alert. Himmler's SS was busily organizing the "incident" planned to start the war.

It was too late for Chamberlain to pen a personal letter to Hitler in which he declared: "Whatever may prove to be the nature of the German-Soviet Agreement, it cannot alter Great Britain's obligation to Poland. . . ."

It was too late for the French ambassador in Berlin to warn Hitler that "if Poland is attacked, France will be at the side of Poland with all its forces."

It was too late for the German conspirators against Hitler to do more than indulge in endless talk and idle plans.

On the evening of August 31, 1939, Der Fuehrer made his last lying peacetime speech to the German people. He ranted about how he had offered peace proposals to Poland and had them rejected (this was a lie—he had seen to it that neither the Polish nor the Allied governments had even had time to read, let alone reply to, his "peace proposals") and about his duty to "protect" the German minority against Polish persecution in Danzig and Poland. Even as he was speaking over Berlin Radio, Hitler knew that SS men dressed in Polish uniforms were blowing up the German radio station at Gleiwitz. And even before this "incident" could be made known to the world, German armies marched. At 4:30 A.M. on September 1, 1939, German mechanized formations poured over the Polish border, thereby plunging the world into the bloodiest war in mankind's long and bloody history.

Within hours of the news of the German attack the British and, later, the French government handed Hitler ultimatums in which they demanded the withdrawal of German troops. Of course such demands were now mere formalities. On September 3, a little after noon, Chamberlain informed the British Parliament that Great Britain was now at war with Germany, as was France.

In Berlin, Hermann Goering, the fat and brutal Chief of the German Air Force, who had done so much to bring this war about, said: "If we lose this war, then God have mercy on us!"

Seven

THE YEARS OF VICTORY

POLAND SUCCUMBED TO THE GERMAN ONSLAUGHT IN eighteen days. One and a half million German troops overwhelmed the 35 Polish divisions (approximately half a million soldiers) in a military disaster such as the world had not seen before. With planes roaring overhead to scout and bomb, whole divisions of tanks and self-propelled artillery raced down the Polish roads at forty miles per hour. Motorized infantry followed them. The Polish Army was split, then split again, and surrounded. It was the world's first taste of *Blitzkrieg* (lightning war). To oppose it, the Poles could muster almost no armor or air power. Their planes had been destroyed in sudden bombing attacks on the dawn of September 1. The Polish Army was not lacking in spirit, it was simply hopelessly outclassed. Polish cavalry units charged with their lances at the ready against German tanks—a brave but utterly futile gesture. Cracow, Poland's second most important city, fell to the Germans on September 6; by September 15 the Polish government had fled Warsaw and reached the Romanian border. And by that date organized Polish resistance had come to an end, except in Warsaw (which surrendered on September 25) and among isolated units which continued fighting with great but useless courage. Then, on September 17—at 6 P.M.—Russia suddenly invaded already defeated Poland from the east.

The Russian decision to jump in on the rape of Poland had been taken some time before, at Germany's urging. Fearful of a French attack from the west, the German generals were desperate to finish off the Polish campaign and begin transferring their armies to the Westwall. For this reason Hitler had urged Stalin not to miss this opportunity to enlarge the Soviet Union at Poland's expense. But the speed of the German advance caught the Russians by surprise. And, besides that, Stalin needed some sort of excuse to offer to the outside world for his cynical aggression. Unfortunately the only excuse the Russian government could dream up was that they were entering eastern Poland in order to protect the White Russian and Ukrainian populations of their districts against Germany—Russia's ally! As Foreign Minister Molotov stated: "This argument was necessary to make the intervention of the Soviet Union plausible to the masses and at the same time avoid giving the Soviet Union the appearance of an aggressor."

In any event, the Russian attack, while it was too late to contribute to the German victory, did ensure the total subjugation of the Polish nation. The Russian troops advanced to the Curzon Line, so named for the British statesman who had drawn it in 1919. To the east of that line most of the population was Russian, to the west Polish. So Stalin could claim with some justification he was only reabsorbing territory which Poland had grabbed in 1920. More than that, it ensured that the overwhelming majority of rebellious Poles would be left on Germany's hands. By the end of September, too, Stalin had taken over the small Baltic nations of Latvia, Estonia, and Lithuania. All of this was the payment Russia had demanded from Germany in August in return for the Nazi-Soviet Nonaggression Pact which made Hitler's war possible. Der Fuehrer paid the price willingly enough for the time being. He was still determined to prevent a two-front war, and accounts had not yet been settled with the British and French. To that task Hitler now addressed himself.

As early as September 6, with the Polish Army destroyed, German divisions had begun to shift to the Western Front. But during most of September only 23 German divisions of poor quality faced the 110 French and British divisions. As General Alfred Jodl testified later at Nuremberg: "If the French had . . . used the engagement of the German forces in Poland, they would have been able to cross the Rhine without our being able to prevent it and would have threatened the Ruhr area, which was the most decisive factor of the German conduct of the war."

But the Western Front was strangely quiet, German and French troops facing each other in the Siegfried and Maginot Lines, respectively, hardly fired a shot. The British Royal Air Force was requested by their French allies to refrain from bombing German targets, for fear of retaliation from Hitler's Luftwaffe. But Hitler had no intention of unleashing the fury of air attack against his enemies just yet. On September 7, at a conference with his commanders, Hitler directed that "my express command must be obtained . . . every time one of our planes crosses the western borders; [and] for every air attack on Britain." So quiet was the Western Front that Germans soon nicknamed the war in the west the *Sitzkrieg* (sit-down war) while in Britain it was known as the "phony war." Not that Britain had many troops to fight in France in any event. By October 11, 1939, only 4 British divisions were to be found in France.

Why didn't the French, with their overwhelmingly superior army, attack in September? There were many

reasons. The French High Command was infected by
defeatism; they were sure they would lose any open engagement against the German Army. And by mid-Sep-
tember, when French mobilization was more or less
complete, Poland had been defeated. To attack then
would not help the Poles. But mainly the French were
terrified of another bloodletting such as they had experienced during the First World War. An entire French
generation had been wiped out at places like the
Somme and Verdun. French manpower was woefully
inadequate in the younger age groups. Proportionately,
no nation had suffered so much from World War I (except possibly Russia), and the people of France were
determined to avoid the horrors of another war like
that. This defeatism found expression in French political life at the highest level and even led many important
French officials to commit acts for which they were
later to be condemned for high treason.

As for Hitler, by not attacking in the west he hoped
to persuade the Allies to conclude peace now that Poland was destroyed. He took the lack of an Allied offensive (correctly) as a sign that the Western powers were
not really determined to fight a full-scale war against
Germany. On October 6, speaking before his personal
collection of Nazi party hacks in the Reichstag, Hitler
made an open appeal for peace. "Why should this war
in the west be fought?" he demanded. "For restoration
of Poland? Poland . . . will never rise again. What
other reason exists?"

But by that time Der Fuehrer had already decided on
a brutal offensive in the west. His long-winded and confused directives now began to descend once again upon
the General Staff and the Army Supreme Command. A
plan which called for the main German attack to be
made through Belgium, as in World War I, was de-
vised. And an attack date of November 12, 1939, was
set. This date was later to be postponed no less than

sixteen times—but the driving intention behind it never changed.

As early as October 10, 1939, Grand Admiral Erich Raeder had stressed to Hitler the advantages of securing Norwegian bases for his submarines. Operating from northern waters, the German undersea fleet would easily break through the British blockade. But of more decisive importance to German calculations was the fact that German industry depended upon Swedish iron ore. This ore, which was transported across the Baltic Sea to Germany during the summer months, had to be shipped down the exposed Norwegian Atlantic coast during the winter. Only the fact that German freighters were inside Norwegian territorial waters all the way saved them from British air and sea attack. But would the British continue to respect Norwegian neutrality? If not, the consequences to German industry would be catastrophic. Then, on November 30, 1939, Russia attacked Finland. The British and French started to organize an expeditionary force to go to the aid of the hard-pressed Finns. But this force would have to go through Norway and Sweden to reach Finland. And Hitler had little doubt that, once embarked, the Allies would seize the opportunity to cut off German iron ore imports. On March 3, 1940, he decided that the seizure of Norway and Denmark must precede his attack in the west.

Following a precise plan and a carefully worked-out timetable, German forces (5 divisions were used) under the command of General Nikolaus von Falkenhorst put to sea on April 7 in freighters guarded by German cruisers and destroyers. Their objectives were Copenhagen, the Danish capital (other German forces were to cross the land frontier of that country), and the Norwegian ports of Narvik, Trondheim, Stavanger, Bergen—and the Norwegian capital, Oslo. Everything depended on speed and secrecy. For if the British should catch the German ships at sea, or even if the Norwegian coastal forts should open fire on them, catastrophe might ensue. But in spite of warnings from anti-Nazi conspirators on the German General Staff, the Norwegians, Danes, and British were unprepared for this daring assault.

On the morning of April 9, while German troops were disembarking from the hold of a German freighter in Copenhagen and other forces were pouring over the Danish border, the German ambassador informed King Christian X that his small country was being taken "under the protection" of Germany. Resistance was hopeless, and after a few shots had been fired, King Christian and his government surrendered to the Nazis.

The Germans got a far different reception in Norway on that morning of April 9. Norwegian guns on two ancient and rusting ironclads in Narvik harbor opened fire as soon as the German flotilla of ten destroyers and a troopship appeared. The Norwegian ships were quickly sunk and Narvik seized by two battalions of German troops. Trondheim, where resistance was also offered, was taken almost as easily. At Bergen, Norwegian shore batteries badly damaged the German cruiser *Koenigsberg,* but the city was conquered anyhow by German troops put ashore by other vessels. Later that same day 15 British naval dive bombers appeared and sank the *Koenigsberg* in Bergen harbor. At Oslo, the Germans ran into real trouble. The German troop convoy, led by the pocket battleship *Luetzow* (formerly the *Deutschland,* its name had been changed by Hitler for fear of losing a ship with the name "Germany") and the brand-new heavy cruiser *Bluecher,* had to sail up a 50-mile fjord to reach its objective. Fifteen miles below Oslo the Norwegian coastal fortress of Oskarsborg opened fire and sank the *Bluecher* and badly damaged the *Luetzow.* The German convoy turned back, but Oslo was captured the next day by German parachutists. King Haakon VII of Norway (the brother of Denmark's Christian X) and his government fled to the Norwegian mountains in the north. From there they hurled defiance at the German invaders and tried to rally their three million countrymen to fight against the might of the Third Reich. Norwegian resistance on the first day of invasion had been, to some extent, sabotaged by the activities of one Vidkum Quisling and his followers. Quisling, a former Norwegian Minister of Defense and long-time Nazi, never was to have much influence either with Norwegians or with Germans, though the Nazis named him head of a Norwegian captive government. But his name entered most of the languages of the world—meaning traitor.

On April 5, while the first German naval supply ships were leaving German harbors for Norway, Prime Minister Chamberlain had said in a speech that because the Germans had failed to attack in the west while the Allies were unready, "Hitler has missed the bus." This memorable phrase was to haunt the Allies for the next several weeks—beginning in Norway. Although a British destroyer flotilla (backed by the old battleship *Warspite*) sank all the ten German destroyers at Narvik and landed a British force which drove the two Nazi battalions to the hills, the British effort in Norway was a case of "too little and too late," as Churchill later admitted. The British fleet could not operate effectively in Norwegian waters because of German Air Force strength, which was now established in Norway itself, and British forces landed near Trondheim found themselves outnumbered and underequipped. By May 2 all of southern Norway was in German hands. It seemed for a while that the strong Allied force at Narvik would be able to hold out and to cut off German iron ore, thereby undermining Hitler's main reason for attacking Scandinavia. But by June the Germans had struck with terrible strength on the Western Front, and every Allied soldier was needed to help stop them. The Narvik force was reembarked and returned to England. On June 7 King Haakon and his government also fled to England and the fighting in Norway came to an end.

The German plan of attack in the west had undergone drastic revisions during the winter of 1939–40. In place of the original intention to make the main push through Belgium as in 1914, the Germans had adopted a new and daring plan put forward by General Fritz von Manstein, a junior General Staff officer. Von Manstein's plan was to invade Belgium and Holland with only light forces. The British and French, assuming that the Germans were attacking in force there, would rush their armies to meet them. Then the main German thrust, composed almost entirely of armored tank divisions and motorized infantry, would strike through the Ardennes, south of the French-Belgian border. The heavily wooded Ardennes would be difficult terrain for tanks. But surprise would be on the German side. And once the armored divisions had broken through, they could turn north into good tank country and head for the Channel, thereby trapping the British and French armies which had raced into Belgium. To carry out this plan the Germans had 135 divisions to the 136 British, French, Belgian and Dutch divisions. But at the Ardennes, weakly held by French troops, the Germans could mass 7 heavy armored divisions, followed by light tank divisions and divisions of motorized infantry. The German striking column waiting to attack through this hilly and wooded region stretched back for more than a hundred miles into Germany!

On May 10, 1940, the Germans struck in Belgium and Holland. The Dutch resisted heroically for a few days, but after Rotterdam had been subjected to a mass air raid by the Luftwaffe that destroyed the center of the city, and with German troops pouring into

the tiny country, the Dutch were overwhelmed. Queen
Wilhelmina and her government escaped aboard two
British destroyers. It was all over in exactly four days.
Belgium held out a little longer. True to the German
General Staff's predictions, as soon as the Germans attacked Belgium and Holland, the British and French
armies had rushed forward to meet what they thought
to be the main German thrust. But on May 14 the
German armored column waiting at the Ardennes
crashed into France. Preceded by Stuka dive bombers
which screamed down out of the sky and by waves of
fighters and fighter-bombers, the huge mass of swift-
moving armor destroyed everything in its path, racing
north toward the Channel to trap the Allied armies in
Belgium. By May 20 the German tanks had reached
Abbeville on the Channel and the Belgians, the British
Expeditionary Force of six divisions, and three French
armies were trapped. Four days later the Allied forces
had been compressed into a tiny triangle around the
small port of Dunkirk. And then—just as all seemed
lost—the German forces inexplicably halted.

There were several reasons why the victorious German armies were halted short of their goal. For one
thing, conservative General Staff officers were worried
that the tanks and men had outraced their supplies.
More important than that, Hermann Goering, jealous
of the Army's great victories, wanted to gain glory for
his Air Force. He convinced Hitler that the Luftwaffe
would be sufficient to destroy the trapped Anglo-
French forces and to prevent any evacuation by sea.
Perhaps more important still was Hitler's conviction
that Britain would soon surrender. With victory in his
grasp, Der Fuehrer did not want to inflict the terrible
humiliation of capturing the entire BEF upon Great
Britain—if he did that, he feared that the English
would never surrender. That his line of reasoning in
this respect was nonsensical is obvious. While the Ger-

man generals fumed and fretted within sight of their goal, the British organized a mass evacuation of the Allied forces such as the world had never seen before. The "miracle of Dunkirk" was an expression of the will of an entire people. While the Royal Navy took off as many men as it could, hundreds and hundreds of ordinary Englishmen sailed their private boats across the inferno of the Channel to rescue as many men as they could carry. Overhead, the Royal Air Force made a desperate and successful effort to obtain local air supremacy. Goering's vaunted Luftwaffe was held at bay as, from the raging chaos of Dunkirk, 338,226 men were carried to safety in England—men who had lost their weapons, but men who would live to fight and win another day. By June 4 it was all over. When the German armored columns finally reached Dunkirk that day, their prey had eluded them.

Great Britain's plight was grim indeed. Although many of her best-trained and battle-tested troops had been saved from German captivity, the BEF was shattered. Weapons were so short that thousands of men had no rifles. President Franklin D. Roosevelt had to strip American armories of their old-fashioned Springfield rifles and rush them secretly to England in a desperate effort to rearm the British forces, even with antiquated weapons. But England had at last found leadership worthy of her people. The aged and fumbling Chamberlain had been replaced on May 10 by the energetic and brilliant Winston Churchill as Prime Minister. Churchill, who had recognized the Hitler menace from the very beginning, was a born fighter, an experienced strategist, a daring leader, and a statesman of tremendous stature. He was also perhaps the greatest orator the English language has ever known. He was able to marshal words which could arouse not only his own countrymen but freedom-loving peoples everywhere. When on that black June 4, with Great

Britain almost defenseless before the massed might of Germany, he arose to address Parliament, his words rang like a trumpet call around the world:

"Even though large tracts of Europe and many old and famous states have fallen or may fall into the grip of the Gestapo and all the odious apparatus of Nazi rule, we shall not flag or fail. We shall go on to the end, we shall fight in France, we shall fight in the seas and oceans, we shall fight with growing confidence and growing strength in the air, we shall defend our island whatever the cost may be, we shall fight on the beaches, we shall fight on the landing grounds, we shall fight in the fields and in the streets, we shall fight in the hills; we shall never surrender, and even if, which I do not for a moment believe, this island or a large part of it were subjugated and starving, then our Empire beyond the seas, armed and guarded by the British Fleet, would carry on the struggle, until, in God's good time, the New World, with all its power and might, steps forth to the rescue and liberation of the Old."

Churchill's defiance was dismissed in Berlin as the death rattle of the British Empire. It was to take Hitler a long time to realize that in Churchill he was faced with an enemy who, more than any other single individual, would bring about his downfall. But Der Fuehrer's optimism seemed well-founded in June 1940. The heavy German armor, its task in the north completed, turned now to crush the remnants of the French Army. On June 14, German troops marched into Paris and the swastika flag was hoisted to the top of the Eiffel Tower. Only four days earlier Mussolini, anxious to get in on the spoils, had entered the war on Germany's side. The contempt which his actions aroused in the rest of the world was well-expressed by President Roosevelt, who declared: "The hand that held the dagger has now plunged it into the back of its neighbor." But it was a very small dagger. Even with the French Army reeling in defeat, Mussolini's troops could make no headway at all in their attack in the south. But the defeatism and demoralization which had for so many years undermined the French national will now found its ultimate expression in the person of Marshal Henri Pétain, who was named Premier of a defeated and prostrate France and who, on June 17, asked the Germans for an armistice. On June 21, French negotiators accepted the German armistice terms in the same railroad car in the forest of Compiègne in which Marshal Foch had dictated peace to the Emperor's emissaries in 1918. The French humiliation and Hitler's vengeful joy were both complete.

With German arms triumphant from Warsaw to the Atlantic and from Norway to the Spanish border, Hitler now once again offered England peace. He was willing to leave the British Empire intact; in fact, even to "guarantee" it. England's position was hopeless and he wished to spare her the horrors of a German invasion, he said.

But on June 18, after France had already asked for an armistice, Churchill once again addressed Parliament and insisted that Britain would carry on the war no matter what terrors the Germans might unleash. "Let us therefore brace ourselves to our duties," he said, "and so bear ourselves that, if the British Empire and its Commonwealth last for a thousand years, men will say: 'This was their finest hour.' "

Hitler was now faced with a problem which was to prove insoluble. In order to bring the war to an end he would have to conquer England. But in order to do that he would have to invade the British Isles or so terrorize the English people through air attack that they would be willing to surrender. The German Navy, however, was under no illusions that it could hope to transport a German Army across the Channel. Hitler's plan to invade England—named "Operation Sea Lion"—upon which the German General Staff expended much energy during July and August of 1940 always came up against the hard fact that the Royal Navy was very much in command of the sea. Nor did the Germans possess the specialized landing craft which would be necessary, or any experience of seaborne assault. The German plan called for transporting 260,000 men across the choppy Channel in barges and tugs over a period of three days. Airborne units were to seize certain airfields behind the beachheads. Once the landings were secured, German forces were expected to conquer England in less than a month. There is much evidence that neither Hitler nor the German General Staff ever took Operation Sea Lion seriously. If they had attempted such an invasion, it would almost certainly have turned into a disaster for the Germans. We now know that the British had planned to throw the entire might of the Royal Navy into the Channel, greet the landing barges with seas of flaming gasoline, use mustard gas on the beachheads, and concentrate 35 divisions against any assault forces which might have survived this reception. Although tentative dates for Operation Sea Lion and even preliminary preparations such as the gathering of troops in the French and Belgian Channel ports and the transferring of barges to the Channel coast were undertaken, most German generals and Hitler himself seem to have regarded these measures more as political than military threats.

But if Germany lacked the means to invade Britain, what of the other alternative—the destruction of British industry and the terrorizing of her population through air power? Hermann Goering, in spite of the Luftwaffe's failure to destroy the British at Dunkirk, assured Der Fuehrer that his mighty Air Force could sweep the Royal Air Force from the skies and bring

England to her knees. If the RAF could be vanquished and British industry wiped out, perhaps a cross-Channel invasion might not be necessary or, if still necessary, might have much greater prospects of success. Hitler agreed and, on August 15, 1940, unleashed the Luftwaffe in what was to become known as the Battle of Britain.

For the next three weeks an aerial war such as the world had never seen raged over England. The Luftwaffe, intent on its primary task of destroying the RAF, sent wave after wave of hundreds of fighters and bombers—sometimes flying 1,200 missions in a single day—to destroy English airfields, radar stations, aircraft factories, and command posts. RAF fighter planes were to be "lured" into combat with the mighty German formations and destroyed. But the RAF needed no luring. Day after day the badly outnumbered English fighters roared from their bomb-battered fields to strike at the German air fleets. And it was soon apparent that the British Spitfire and Hurricane fighters were more than a match for the German Messerschmitts. Besides that, the British fighter command employed radar to locate and track the German planes, and radar was something for which the Germans were unprepared in 1940 and which they did not fully understand. Yet in spite of heavy German losses, which mounted to scores of planes in a single day, the German superiority in numbers began to tell. By September 6, the English were throwing their last fighter reserves into the battle. But the Germans did not realize that. They knew only that their losses were now mounting beyond the thousand mark and still the dogged English fighters refused to be beaten. On September 7, Goering made a fatal mistake. On that day he ordered his battered Luftwaffe to turn from daylight attack against the RAF to night terror raids over English cities.

Every night, during the terrible week that followed, hundreds of German bombers loosed their loads of death and destruction onto London. Large parts of the city were wiped out, over a thousand civilians were killed, thousands were wounded, and many more thousands were made homeless. Certain sections of London were turned into a sea of flames. It seemed that no city population could take such punishment and survive. But Londoners proved they were made of stern stuff. Far from being cowed by the German terror raids, they simply grew more determined to win through to final victory.

On September 15, confident that the air war over Britain was won, Goering ordered a massive daylight raid on London. But the RAF was waiting. That day the English fighters shot down so many German bombers and fighters that the Luftwaffe never even reached its target. The air battle of September 15 was one of the decisive turning points in the war. For on that day the Germans realized that they could not hope to win air supremacy over the British Isles. Therefore invasion was out of the question. And while night terror raids were to continue to obliterate huge sections of London and provincial cities such as Coventry and Birmingham, bringing death and misery to the English people in the months ahead, the Nazis had lost their first battle. More than that, the Luftwaffe was never to recover fully from the terrible beating it took in the skies over England. The courage and sacrifice of a mere handful of English fighter pilots had stopped the mighty German war machine dead in its tracks. As Churchill declared of the RAF: "Never in the field of human conflict was so much owed by so many to so few."

But while Hitler carried on his losing assault against the British Isles, he had not forgotten Germany's target number one—Russia. For in spite of the Nazi-Soviet treaty, Der Fuehrer had always planned on turning eventually to conquest of the east. Only by carving out huge territories in Russia, he believed, could Germany gain the "living space" it needed to expand. This had been a major theme in *Mein Kampf* and, as we have seen, had formed a basic pattern of German history since earliest times. As early as August 1940, with the air war still raging over England, Hitler had ordered his generals to plan for an attack on the Soviet Union sometime in the spring of 1941. On August 14, for example, Hermann Goering had informed his economic aides that delivery of manufactured goods to the Russians by the terms of the Soviet-German Trade Agreement would be discontinued in the spring of 1941. On August 26, Hitler ordered 12 divisions transferred from France to Poland and inaugurated a secret buildup of forces in the east.

Hitler's immediate justification for turning on Russia was that as long as the Soviet Union remained a power factor in Europe, the embattled British would entertain hopes that one day the Red Army might strike at Germany. By destroying Russia, Hitler argued, he would wipe out England's last hope of defeating Germany and bring about her surrender. Besides that, the Russians, by seizing the Baltic states, waging war against Finland, and grabbing the former Russian province of Bessarabia from Romania, were in effect blackmailing Germany. To all this Der Fuehrer determined to put an end. Plans for the invasion of Russia, under the code name of "Operation Barbarossa," were carefully worked out by the General Staff all during the late fall and early winter of 1940.

On September 27, 1940, the representatives of Germany, Italy, and Japan met in Berlin to sign the Tripartite Pact. By its terms, if any of the signatories were to be attacked by "a third party" the others would rush to her assistance. The "third party" in question was obviously the United States—or it might be Russia. In any event, Stalin's suspicions were aroused sufficiently for Hitler to decide it would be worthwhile to soothe Russian feelings. For this reason Soviet Foreign Minister Vyacheslav Molotov was invited to Berlin for discussions. The tough Russian minister arrived in Berlin on November 12, 1940, full of suspicious questions regarding German intentions in Europe, especially Eastern Europe. German Foreign Minister von Ribbentrop, and Hitler himself, tried to sidetrack the Russian with vague talk about dividing up the world into spheres of influence between Germany, Italy, Russia, and Japan. But the skeptical Molotov insisted on discussing concrete and immediate problems closer to home. So insistent was the Soviet minister that Hitler, who had never been spoken to like that before, was stunned by the hail of probing questions. To divert Molotov, Hitler said: "After the conquest of England, the British Empire would be apportioned as a gigantic worldwide estate in bankruptcy of forty million square kilometers." And in dividing up these immense spoils, Russia would receive her share. But Molotov would not be distracted. The conversation grew tense—and then the air-raid sirens began to wail.

Ribbentrop, Molotov, and the lesser dignitaries scuttled down to an air-raid shelter. There, while the RAF roared above them, the German Foreign Minister turned again to the theme of how the British Empire was to be divided among the victorious dictators. And he insisted to Molotov that the English were decisively beaten. The exasperated Russian Foreign Minister snapped: "If that is so, why are we in the shelter, and whose are these bombs which fall?"

But even while Hitler negotiated with the Russians his plans against them went forward. On December 18, 1940, Der Fuehrer issued a general directive to his top commanders in which May 15, 1941, was set as the date for commencing the invasion of the Soviet Union. The general aim of the invasion would be to destroy the Russian Army in western Russia and drive the heavy German armored forces swiftly forward so that by the end of summer they would hold a line on the Volga River—conquering all of European Russia and being then in a good position to fend off any future Russian attacks from Asia. Two Army groups were to jump off from Poland. One of them would drive on Leningrad, the other on Moscow. A third Army group would invade Russia from the south, driving for Kiev and the Caucasus. One hundred sixty German divisions were to be thrown into this attack (60 divisions being left to defend Europe against British attack). German General Staff estimates of Russian strength at this time were, like those of every other nation, remarkably ill-informed. The German planners figured that no more than 75 Russian divisions of any fighting worth would be opposing them. The general appraisal of the Red Army's ability had fallen also because of its poor performance during the Russo-Finnish War. But while the German buildup for Operation Barbarossa proceeded, Hitler's attention was distracted by the stupidity and weakness of his Italian ally.

Mussolini, jealous of all the glory Der Fuehrer had gained by his conquests in Europe, decided, in the autumn of 1940, that he too could be a conqueror. Accordingly, on October 28, 1940, he ordered the Italian armies in conquered Albania to attack Greece. "Fuehrer," he told the surprised Hitler, "we are on the march! Victorious Italian troops crossed the Greco-Albanian border at dawn today!" Unfortunately for Mussolini's martial reputation the "victorious" Italian troops ran into a stone wall of Greek resistance. Within a week the Italians, utterly defeated by the tough Greek troops, ran back across the Albanian border, and the conquering Greeks threatened to drive them into the sea. More than that, the large Italian Army in Africa, which had made a halfhearted invasion of Egypt, was now set upon by the tiny British dessert forces—and enveloped in disaster. At a cost of 500 men killed, the British drove the Italians halfway across Italian Libya, capturing 130,000 prisoners, 1,250 guns, and 500 tanks. Nor was the Italian homeland safe from attack. On the night of November 11, 1940, Royal Navy bombers from the aircraft carrier *Illustrious* attacked the Italian fleet at Taranto and mauled it so badly that it was effectively put out of action for many months.

Hitler was enraged by the meddling of Mussolini and by the strategic dangers the Italian defeats brought upon his own plans. For if British troops were to join the Greeks, then the RAF would be able to operate from Greek bases and attack the Romanian oilfields on which Hitler's armies depended. Also, the Greeks and British might form a common front in the Balkans and disturb his planned attack on Russia. The German Army would have to pull Mussolini's chestnuts out of the fire for him. Accordingly, German Army units were massed in Bulgaria (which now became Germany's ally) for a descent on Greece. German pressure was also brought to bear on the government of Yugoslavia to persuade them to cooperate with the German attack. But as soon as Yugoslav negotiators concluded an agreement with Der Fuehrer, the people of Yugoslavia's capital, Belgrade, rose up in revolt, overthrew the government, and declared Yugoslavia's determination to maintain her independence.

The news of events in Yugoslavia reached Hitler on March 27, 1941. He flew into a violent rage—one of the most hysterical of his life. He screamed that he would destroy Yugoslavia and would not waste time sending an ultimatum. Hermann Goering was ordered on the spot to use his Luftwaffe to "destroy Belgrade in attacks by waves." Plans for a land attack were hurriedly made—and Operation Barbarossa, the planned attack on Russia, was *postponed by four weeks*. This decision, reached in the heat of anger, was perhaps the most fatal of all Hitler's mistakes.

At dawn on April 6, 1941, German armies poured into Yugoslavia and Greece. Belgrade, as Hitler had ordered, was destroyed. The Luftwaffe, unopposed in the air or even by antiaircraft fire, bombed mercilessly for three days and nights: 17,000 civilians were killed in these attacks and the city reduced to rubble. By April 17 the Yugoslav Army had surrendered; by April 27 the Greeks also surrendered. A small British Expeditionary Force which had been rushed in to help the Greeks was forced to evacuate in a minor Dunkirk. Nor had Der Fuehrer neglected Africa. Although he was too stupid to understand the strategic advantages of exerting the slight effort it would have cost to capture Suez and drive the British from the Middle East, Hitler did send a German armored division to bolster the sagging Italians in Libya. The Italian-German Army in Africa, now placed under the command of General Erwin Rommel, drove the small British forces back into Egypt and, by the end of May 1941 had endangered the entire British position at Suez. But Rommel was never to receive the reinforcements and supplies he needed to win a decisive victory in Africa because Hitler felt that they could not be spared from his major operation—the attack on Russia.

It was because of the imminence of this attack that Rudolf Hess, Hitler's old crony of the Beer Hall *Putsch* days, and head of the Nazi party organization, flew alone in a Messerschmitt fighter plane to Scotland on May 10, 1941. The muddled and dimwitted Hess imagined that he could negotiate with English "friends" to arrange peace between Germany and England while Germany attacked Russia. Hitler had no foreknowledge of his flight and was embarrassed and enraged by it. The British, on the other hand, quickly locked Hess up as a prisoner of war and issued an urgent warning to Stalin to expect a German attack in the near future. But the Soviet dictator turned a deaf ear to this information. Up to the last minute the Russian government clung to the illusion that somehow they might escape Hitler's wrath.

At 3:30 A.M. on June 22, 1941, the mighty German war machine crashed over the Russian borders. Directed personally by Hitler from his new command post, an underground headquarters known as *Wolfsschanze* (Wolf's Lair) in a gloomy East Prussian forest, the heavy German armored forces, motorized infantry, and screaming Luftwaffe dive bombers roared into Russia, chewing up Russian armies in a *blitzkrieg* such as they had inflicted on France. Within three weeks the Germans had advanced 450 miles, destroyed countless Russian divisions, and were now threatening both Leningrad and Moscow. So perfectly according to plan did the Germans advance that both Hitler and the General Staff were confident on July 14 that the war against Russia was basically won—only mopping-up operations would remain. By October 3, 1941, Hitler was proclaiming in Berlin: "I declare today, and I declare it without any reservations, that the enemy in the east has been struck down and will never rise again."

And indeed it seemed that Hitler's boast was well-founded. In spite of the fact that Russian divisions continued to materialize out of thin air, in spite of the fact that Winston Churchill declared that Great Britain would fight side by side as an ally of Soviet Russia (which had done so much to bring England to the verge of defeat), in spite of the fact that American Lend-Lease military supplies which had been flowing to England now began also to go to the Soviet Union, as the winter of 1941 approached it appeared that

Russian resistance could not last much longer. In the south, German armies had captured Kiev, sealed off the Crimea, and seized the Donetz Basin, where 60 percent of Russian industry was concentrated. Leningrad was closely besieged, and Moscow was now only 40 miles from the German front lines. By the middle of October 1941, Hitler's conquests had reached their zenith. German troops stood guard over conquered Europe from Moscow to Paris, from the top of Norway to Greece. And beneath the victorious swastika banners an entire continent sank into a night of German barbarism and savagery without parallel in all history. Hitler called it his "New Order" in Europe, but to civilized men everywhere there were no words adequate to describe the bestial horror of it.

Eight

THE NEW ORDER IN EUROPE

BEHIND THE VICTORIOUS GERMAN ARMIES, IN THE GRIP of Heinrich Himmler's dread SS and Gestapo, Germany had instituted a reign of terror over the lands she had conquered. Basically, the Nazi aim was a German-ruled Europe which would be ruthlessly exploited for the benefit of the German "master race," whose populations would literally be slaves of the Third Reich. Jews, Slavs, and other "subhumans" were to be simply exterminated. The industry of Europe was to produce only for the benefit of Germany while the wealth of the Continent was to be looted and carried to the German homeland. Large areas of Europe were to be annexed directly to Germany and their peoples expelled or exterminated to provide room for German settlers. Other areas in which slave populations might be permitted to exist would be ruled more or less directly from Berlin through puppet governments.

As early as September of 1939, when German troops crushed Poland, the Nazi terror followed the armies. The administration of the conquered land was placed under a governor general named Hans Frank, a lawyer who had joined the Nazi party in 1927. The aim of his

administration was stated by the Governor General on the day after he took office: "The Poles," he said, "shall be the slaves of the German Reich." In line with this policy, all Polish leaders were to be killed, and those classes of Polish life from which future leaders might arise were to be wiped out. This included the Polish Catholic clergy, the middle classes, and all Poles who had received more than a primary school education. The men capable of leadership in Poland had to be liquidated, Hitler had declared, and those following them had to be eliminated in their turn. Nor was there any need to burden Germany with this. No need at all —they could be murdered right there in Poland. The executions which followed killed tens of thousands of Poles whose only crime was the fact that they had some education.

Heinrich Himmler, who had been placed in charge of clearing Polish land for German settlers, evicted 1.2 million Poles and over 300,000 Jews from the territory west of the Vistula River to make way for 500,000 German settlers. The mass deportations, which were carried out in the severe winter of 1939–40, cost untold thousands of lives. Later, boasting of his accomplishment, Himmler would recall: "In Poland, in weather forty degrees below zero, we had to haul away thousands, tens of thousands, hundreds of thousands; we had to have the toughness . . . to shoot thousands of leading Poles. . . . Gentlemen, it is much easier in many cases to go into combat . . . than to carry out executions or to haul away people or to evict crying and hysterical women."

It was in Poland, too, that the first of the German extermination camps was constructed. These places of horror differed from concentration camps in that some few people actually survived life in concentration camps —but none were to emerge from the extermination camps.

The fate of Russia was to be the same as that of Poland. By special order of Der Fuehrer, all Jews and Russian political commissars found in the ranks of the prisoners of war were to be immediately shot. Special Action Groups, formed of SS thugs, were to follow the German armies and exterminate Jews, Soviet leaders, and educated Russians. Ranging far and wide behind the German armies, these Special Action Groups murdered over 630,000 men, women, and children, mostly Jews, during the German occupation of Russia.

The Nazi attitude toward conquered Europe was summed up by Himmler in a talk he gave to SS officers on October 4, 1943. "What the nations can offer in the way of good blood of our type," he said, "we will take, if necessary by kidnaping their children and raising them here with us. Whether nations live in prosperity or starve to death like cattle interests me only in so far as we need them as slaves to our way of life."

Hermann Goering, as director of the German economy, was equally frank as to what he intended to do in the conquered lands. "It used to be called plundering," he said on August 6, 1942, "but today things have become more humane. In spite of that, I intend to plunder and to do it thoroughly."

After each conquest of a foreign country Nazi financial agents seized all the gold they could find in its banks. Then tremendous "occupation costs" would be imposed on the population. It was estimated that Germany took two thirds of the national incomes of Belgium and Holland in this manner. France was forced to pay *four times* as much yearly reparations to Germany as Germany had been forced to pay under the much-hated Versailles Treaty. But this monetary looting was slight compared to the plundering of national industries. Hundreds of factories in the conquered lands were dismantled and shipped to Germany, while agricultural output was seized for German consumption. From

France alone about 75 percent of French grain production was stolen. That such robberies would leave conquered populations to starve was no concern of the Germans.

But harsh as German economic exploitation was, the exploitation of human beings under the German slave-labor program was far worse. By the end of 1944 there were more than 7.5 million slaves toiling in German factories, homes, and on German farms. Most of these people had been rounded up by the SS at gunpoint, stuffed into boxcars, and shipped like cattle to Germany. Wives and husbands and children were separated and sent to toil in different places. Children old enough to work were kidnaped in mass raids. Thus in occupied Russia, according to a memorandum found among the captured German documents, "Army Group Center intends to apprehend forty to fifty thousand youths from the age of 10 to 14 . . . and transport them to the Reich. It is intended to allot these juveniles primarily to the German trades as apprentices."

None of the conquered peoples anywhere in Europe could ever be sure they would not be seized for labor in Germany at any time. They might be grabbed as they came out of churches or movie theaters, or the SS might simply block off an entire area of a city or a whole town and round up every able-bodied person they came across.

German businessmen and industrialists made ruthless use of this slave labor. The giant Krupp armament works, for example, employed thousands of slaves. The conditions under which they lived were described by Dr. Wilhelm Jaeger, the doctor assigned to Krupp's slaves. There were no medical supplies. The slave laborers had no shoes and only a sack for clothing. There was little food and less sanitation. The slave workers were dying like flies. In another of the Krupp work camps Dr. Jaeger found that the workers had been kept for nearly half a year in dog kennels, urinals, and old baking houses. The dog kennels were three feet high, nine feet long and six feet wide. Five men slept in each of them.

In case any of these slaves showed signs of rebellion Himmler directed that "special treatment is requested." Special treatment was hanging.

For those slaves who worked on German farms, life was little better. A German government directive declared: "The farm workers have to labor as long as is demanded by the employer." There were no time limits to the working time. Every employer had the right to beat his workers. They could be kept in stables and no pity was to be shown them.

As for women who were seized to provide domestic service in German households as maids, cooks, charwomen: "There is no claim to free time. It is prohibited to them to enter restaurants, movies, theaters, and similar establishments. Attending church is also prohibited."

Besides the 7.5 million civilians impressed into slavery in Germany, nearly 3 million prisoners of war were forced to labor in armament factories. But forced labor was the least of their worries. About 5.75 million Russian soldiers became prisoners of war in Germany during the war. Of these less than 1 million survived. The rest were deliberately starved to death, shot en masse, allowed to die of disease. This was not simply because of the difficulty of providing food and care for so many prisoners. It was German policy. Alfred Rosenberg, the muddleheaded Nazi "philosopher," recalled that on the march to the camps, the Russian population was not allowed to give the prisoners food. And often, when the prisoners could no longer keep up on the march because of hunger and exhaustion, they were shot before the eyes of the horrified civilian population and the corpses were left.

Western prisoners of war—especially English and

Americans—received somewhat better treatment. On the other hand, on October 18, 1942, Hitler personally ordered that all Allied commandos falling into German hands be executed to the last man. And, after Allied air raids began to pulverize German cities, the German civilian population was encouraged to lynch airmen who had bailed out over Germany. On one occasion forty-seven American, British, and Dutch fliers were murdered at Mauthausen concentration camp. A French prisoner at the camp described the scene: "The forty-seven officers were led barefooted to the quarry. . . . At the bottom of the steps the guards loaded stones on the backs of these poor men and they had to carry them to the top. The first journey was made with stones weighing about sixty pounds and accompanied by blows. . . . The second journey the stones were still heavier, and whenever the poor wretches sank under their burden they were kicked and hit with a bludgeon . . . in the evening twenty-one bodies were strewn along the road. The twenty-six others died the following morning."

An essential part of the German technique for keeping Europe subdued was the use of terror. Any attack upon a German soldier, any act of sabotage, any sign of resistance was to be punished by the taking and execution of hostages. The proportion proclaimed by the Germans was to be one hundred hostages shot for every German killed. In France 30,000 hostages were executed by the Germans during the war and another 40,000 died in German prisons in France. In Holland 2,000 were killed, in Poland, 8,000. In Denmark, where on Hitler's orders five Danes were to be shot for each German killed, SS troops seized and murdered the great Danish poet-playwright, Karl Munk. His body was found beside a road with a sign pinned to it: "Swine, you worked for Germany just the same."

On December 7, 1941, Hitler issued a decree which

was to be become infamous throughout Europe as the "Night and Fog Decree." This was to be applied to persons anywhere in Europe who might sooner or later endanger German security. To terrorize their families and friends such persons were to be seized by the SS or the Gestapo late at night and hustled away. No word of their fate was ever to reach their families. They were simply to disappear into the night and fog. Even though they were inevitably killed later, no further information about them would ever become known. Untold thousands of Europeans vanished from their homes in this manner, and only a handful ever returned from the "night and fog."

Perhaps the most infamous of all the German acts of terror in Europe was the destruction of the Czech village of Lidice. It was meant to be an object lesson to any who would dare to strike back at the Nazi gangsters. For on May 28, 1942, Reinhard Heydrich— "Hangman Heydrich"—the deputy chief of the Gestapo and Himmler's number two man in the SS, who had been personally responsible for the deaths of untold hundreds of thousands, was killed in Prague. A few days earlier two Czech soldiers of the Free Czech Army in England had been parachuted into Czechoslovakia by the RAF. They were equipped with a bomb and weapons, and their mission was to execute Heydrich, the man who had murdered so many of their people. On May 29 they threw their bomb at him as he drove through Prague in an open sports car. Heydrich's spine was shattered by the blast, and he died six days later. Immediately thousands of Czechs were rounded up and executed by the Gestapo. The two assassins, who had escaped momentarily, were later killed by the SS among hundreds of other victims—the Germans never knew they had killed the assassins. But to the Nazi mind this was not vengeance enough. Therefore, on the morning of June 9, truckloads of Gestapo men surrounded the little Czech village of Lidice. All the men and boys over the age of sixteen in the village were shot. All the women were sent to German concentration camps, where most of them were later murdered. All the children were sent first to concentration camps and then parceled out to German families. Then the village was burned to the ground and every trace of its existence wiped out. Nor, though Lidice was the most famous, was it the only village in Europe to meet this terrible fate. Villages in Poland, Russia, Yugoslavia, Greece, Norway, and France were similarly destroyed.

But terrible as were the crimes committed by Germany against the conquered people, they pale into insignificance compared to the Nazi massacre of Europe's Jews. From the very beginning Hitler had decreed that Europe was to be made "Jew-free." This meant nothing less than the murder of every Jew in every country conquered by Germany. Among the Nazis it was referred to as "the final solution of the Jewish problem." There were 11 million Jews in Europe—and they were all, men, women, and children, marked for death. The attitude of their murderers toward the problems of exterminating them was expressed by Himmler in 1943 in his talk to SS officers on October 4: "I also want to talk to you quite frankly on . . . the extermination of the Jewish race. . . . Most of *you* must know what it means when 100 corpses are lying side by side, or 500, or 1,000. To have stuck it out and at the same time— apart from exceptions caused by human weakness—to have remained decent fellows, that is what has made us hard. This is a page of glory in our history."

In order to handle the tremendous number of people involved, the Germans, with typical thoroughness, built several special extermination camps to "process" their victims. But of all these hideous places Auschwitz, in Poland, was the largest and most efficient. There as many as 6,000 people a day were killed and their bodies cremated.

Jews—men, women, and children of all ages—were rounded up in conquered countries by the Gestapo and the SS. Many of course were murdered immediately (about a million) by shooting, etc. But most were loaded onto boxcars and shipped to the extermination camps in Poland. Often they were told they were being "resettled" in the east. When the trains, after long journeys during which no food or water was provided, arrived at Auschwitz, the surviving victims were herded together at the railroad siding. There several Nazi doctors would examine them. Those who were judged fit for labor were marched away. Of course this meant that families were separated—but every attempt was made to fool the victims into thinking that they would at least survive. Picture postcards were handed out to be signed and sent back home to friends and relatives. Then the Jews were marched over to large chambers surrounded by well-kept lawns and flower gardens, which bore signs reading "Baths." The men, women, and children who had now reached the "bathhouses" were made to undress, handed towels, and told they were about to take a shower. They they were herded into the "shower room"—two thousand at a time—and the doors were locked shut and hermetically sealed. And while the prisoners looked up and wondered why no water came from the "shower" spouts, crystals of hydrogen-cyanide gas were poured into the vents. It usually took twenty to thirty minutes for the people inside to be killed. At the end of that time the gas chamber doors were opened, and men with gas masks entered to take the gold fillings from the teeth of the corpses and to cut off their hair (which was useful to the German economy). Then the bodies were carted over to the specially designed crematorium ovens and burned.

There was no escape from the gas chambers at

Auschwitz for those unfortunate enough to be sent there. Often women would try to hide their children from the SS guards under the piles of clothing—but they were always found and sent into the gas chambers. The children's toys (there were mountains of them) were sent to Germany to gladden the hearts of German children. The gold wrenched from the teeth of the dead was sent for storage to the Reichsbank, Germany's state bank. Clothing and other useful articles were shipped to Germany for sale through pawnshops to German civilians.

And what of those Jews who had been selected for labor rather than the gas chambers on arrival? They were first worked to exhaustion in war plants which had been erected by such companies as Krupp and I. G. Farben Chemicals at the extermination camps—and then sent to the gas chambers.

There was much competition among German companies for contracts in the construction of these extermination centers. In submitting their bids for the building of crematorium ovens, the firm of C. H. Kori, for example, assured the SS: "We guarantee the effectiveness of the cremation ovens, as well as their durability, the use of the best materials and our faultless workmanship."

Over six million Jews were killed by the Nazis throughout Europe—over one million at Auschwitz alone. This gigantic crime required all the tremendous organizing power, technical efficiency, and industriousness for which Germany had so long been famous.

The extermination of the Jews was, by and large, carried out on a national basis. A special section of the SS, under the direction of Adolf Eichmann, handled the rounding up and shipping of the unfortunate people. Eichmann's organization worked one country at a time. Thus most of the Jews in Poland were "processed" before the Nazi thugs turned to France, thence to Belgium, Holland, etc. The Nazis were later to testify that they could not have succeeded in this unprecedented massacre without the cooperation of the Jews themselves. But this was only to say that the Jews had no choice. When they fought—as they bravely did in the Warsaw ghetto, for example—they were simply massacred on the spot by SS units. What is true to say, however, is that these murders could not have been carried out without the at least tacit permission and often the cooperation of the non-Jewish populations of the conquered countries. This was proved by the fate of the Jews in Denmark and in Bulgaria. In Bulgaria, German attempts to even identify Jews were blocked by the interference of the Bulgarian people. When the Germans would have put yellow armbands on the Bulgarian Jews, they found the entire population proudly wearing them; when they would have tried to force the Jews into ghettos and deport them to the extermination centers in Poland, they found their efforts sabotaged.

In Denmark the reaction of the population was so strong that many of the Nazis who were supposedly there to enforce Himmler's orders turned against Hitler's philosophy and took great risks to warn Danes and Danish Jews of German plans to trap them. In the end Hitler had to send regular Army units into Denmark to enforce his orders even among his own administrators. And even then, with the cooperation of certain German officials, the overwhelming majority of Danish Jews were transported across the sea to safety in Sweden. There could be little doubt that where a conquered people was prepared to resist the "final solution to the Jewish problem," that "solution" could not be carried out.

What of the Allies? Could they do nothing to stop the massacre? Both Churchill and Roosevelt issued more than one warning that Germans responsible for atrocities would be brought to justice at the end of the war. And through secret service agents they tried desperately to buy, trade, or negotiate for Jewish lives. In 1944, when he learned that more than half of Hungary's Jews had already been shipped to extermination camps and that the other half were scheduled to follow shortly, President Roosevelt issued a warning to the Hungarian government that if the deportations continued, then "Hungary's fate after the war will be unlike that of any other defeated nation." The deportation of Hungarian Jews stopped at once (although temporarily—they started again in October 1944). But by and large the extent of Hitler's murderous plan was not fully known in the West. Only when advancing British, Russian, and American troops came across the sickening evidence in Germany and Poland did the world realize what had been done. And by then it was too late.

It is, however, both pointless and ironic to try to shift the blame for the destruction of European Jews onto the shoulders of conquered nations or of the Jews themselves. The crime was planned, organized, and carried out by Germany. And if many Germans remained somehow unaware of what their leaders had ordered and what their neighbors, sons, brothers, and husbands were carrying out, there was much evidence to show that many Germans understood only too well. Of course the actual murdering was carried out by psychotic criminals—an element to be found in the population of all countries. But the German people had chosen to follow a leadership which openly proclaimed its intention of loosing such madmen on the world as part of a carefully planned policy of conquest and murder.

Many Germans—especially Army officers—tried later to justify their actions by saying that they were simply following orders as they were duty-bound to do. But by no stretch of any sort of military or civil law, nor any sort of civilized morality, nor any sane conscience, can a man justify brutal murder of the innocent and defenseless on the grounds that someone ordered him to do it. Nor can a sane person even justify closing

his eyes to such crimes and not making every effort to
prevent them. Many Germans would later offer the excuse that if they tried to interfere, they themselves
would be sent to extermination camps. But the worst
that the Nazis could do to a man was to kill him, and
perhaps that might have been preferable to surviving
with a mind poisoned by guilt and a soul tortured by
cowardice. Hans Frank, the Governor General of Poland, who was himself responsible for the atrocious
murder of hundreds of thousands of people—Jews and
non-Jews alike—said, just before he was hanged at Nuremberg: "A thousand years will pass and the guilt of
Germany will not be erased." And for once in his con-
temptible life Frank was right.

The full human impact of what the German policy of
mass murder meant was quietly but overwhelmingly established at the Nuremberg trials after the war, by Sir
Hartley Shawcross, the brilliant British prosecutor.
Summing up the case against the defendants—the top
surviving members of the Hitler government—Sir Hartley read into the record an eyewitness account of a
mass murder by one of Himmler's Special Action Units
in the East:

Without screaming or weeping these people undressed,
stood around in family groups, kissed each other, said
farewells, and waited for a sign from another SS man, who
stood near the pit, also with a whip in his hand. During
the 15 minutes that I stood near I heard no complaint or
plea for mercy. I watched a family of about 8 persons, a
man and a woman, both about 50 with their children of
about 1, 8 and 19, and two grown-up daughters of about
20-24. An old woman with snow-white hair was holding
the one-year-old child in her arms and singing to it and
tickling it. The child was cooing with delight. The couple
were looking on with tears in their eyes. The father was
holding the hand of a boy about ten years old and speak-

ing to him softly; the boy was fighting his tears. The father pointed to the sky, stroked his head and seemed to explain something to him. At that moment the SS man at the pit shouted something to his comrade. The latter counted off about 20 persons and instructed them to go behind the earth mound. Among them was the family which I have mentioned. . . . I walked around the mound and found myself confronted by a tremendous grave. People were closely wedged together and lying on top of each other so that only their heads were visible . . . the pit was already two thirds full. I estimated that it already contained about 1,000 people. I looked for the man who did the shooting. He was an SS man who sat on the edge of the narrow end of the pit, his feet dangling into the pit. He had a tommy gun on his knees and was smoking a cigarette. . . . Then I heard a series of shots . . .

Turning to the French, British, American, and Russian judges, but speaking beyond them in words addressed to all civilized men, Sir Hartley declared:

"You will remember this story when you come to give your decision, but not in vengeance—in a determination that these things shall not occur again. The father—you remember—pointed to the sky, and seemed to say something to his boy."

Nine

THE TURNING OF THE TIDE

When those who read the terrible history of Hitler's Germany look for that exact point at which the Nazi dictator's power began to ebb, when, as Winston Churchill said, "the hinge of fate" began to swing irrevocably against the conquering German hordes, they usually fix upon the great battles of Stalingrad and El Alamein in 1942. But before that, in the late autumn and early winter of 1941, Hitler made two mistakes—one military and the other political—which made eventual German defeat certain. Although there would be great German victories afterwards, there would never again exist the possibility that the Third Reich might somehow win the war or even escape the devastation it had so richly earned.

Hitler's military mistake commenced with a flourish. On September 5, 1941, with the victorious German armies deep inside Russia, and the Red Army beaten and destroyed (as Hitler and his generals imagined), Der Fuehrer ordered one last mighty offensive, which would capture Moscow and bring the Russian state to an end. The attack was to be named "Operation Typhoon" and was to be launched on October 2. Simultaneously, Hitler insisted that other German forces were to capture Leningrad in the north and advance to Stalingrad in the south. When the General Staff protested that Germany simply did not possess enough forces to carry out all these tremendous tasks at once, Hitler flew into a rage and insisted that it be done.

The great German offensive against Moscow followed Napoleon's old route against the Russian capital, and at first it went exceedingly well. Using huge masses of tanks and motorized infantry, the German armies had encircled two Soviet armies and captured 650,000 prisoners by October 15. Five days later German spearheads were within forty miles of Moscow.

Within the Soviet capital, government ministries packed their records and fled. Foreign embassies and their staffs were moved all the way to a temporary capital at Kuibyshev on the Volga River far to the east. But the people of Moscow did not flee. Instead they took up picks and shovels and trudged out to the suburbs to dig trenches and raise whatever barricades they could against the onrushing Germans. To help the Red Army defend their city, men, women, and children worked until they dropped from exhaustion. Many found weapons and formed militia units to fight on the front lines. And, when things looked blackest for them, the Russian weather came to their aid.

The rains—the fearful, torrential Russian rains—started in mid-October. The fields and unpaved roads turned into seas of mud. Hitler's mechanized army was slowed down and then soon stuck fast. Wheeled vehicles sank up to their axles in mud while the infantry slipped and slithered in exhaustion. Tanks sank up to their turrets, supplies took forever to reach the front lines, and, with Moscow in sight, German officers began to recall the fate of Napoleon's mighty army on this same road.

And then came the snow—and the subfreezing temperatures of the bitter Russian winter. On November 3 the first cold wave struck the front. The thermometer fell to below freezing—and kept on dropping. Cases of frostbite among the German troops began to be reported. So confident had Hitler and his generals been of a quick victory over Russia that almost no winter clothing had been provided for the troops. The freezing cold cracked the engine blocks of tanks and trucks, froze up machine guns and rifles, and reduced the unprepared German soldiers to numb misery. Still, at a terrible price, the Germans continued to inch forward. On December 2 a patrol force reached one of Moscow's suburbs. From there they could see the spires of the Kremlin itself. They were driven away, however, by a few tanks and a brigade of factory workers who had been rushed to the danger point. This was to be the closest the Germans would ever get to Moscow.

On December 6, 1941, Russian General Georgi Zhukov struck. Against the exhausted and demoralized Germans he unleashed seven armies and two cavalry corps. Over one hundred divisions of Russian troops especially equipped and trained to fight in the terrible Russian winter weather fell like a thunderbolt on the German armies before Moscow. Neither Hitler nor his generals could imagine where this tremendous force had come from. The Red Army was supposed to be beaten. It had already lost millions of prisoners, thousands of tanks and guns. Yet here were more divisions, more of the deadly Russian T-34 tanks against which German antitank guns were helpless. So tremendous was the Russian assault that the German Army never fully recovered from the blow. During the next weeks, while they retreated over the icy roads (temperatures had now fallen to 30 degrees below zero), it seemed that the whole German front might simply disintegrate. After a long retreat it did not—due to Hitler's fanatical insistence that German troops fight where they stood no matter what the cost (and it was great). But the elite of the German troops and the cream of the German armored divisions were broken. More than that, the myth of German military invincibility was gone, and the self-confidence of the German Army shattered.

If this military debacle in Russia tolled the knell of German conquest and made a long war certain, a political blunder of tremendous magnitude came at the same time to make certain that the war, no matter how long, could never be won by Germany. The political miscalculation was Adolf Hitler's declaration of war against the United States, on December 11, 1941. For if war between Nazi Germany and the American Republic was almost certain in the long run, it was by no means sure that an unprovoked America would have turned its might on the Nazi tyranny at that time.

Although President Franklin D. Roosevelt had recognized the nature of the Nazi threat to American interests as early as 1937, when he made a speech in Chicago urging that the aggressor nations be "quarantined," a very large section of the American people continued to feel that Europe's wars were none of their business. Forming such organizations as "The America-First Committee," which included several U.S. senators and many congressmen, as well as industrialists, newspaper publishers, and other opinion leaders in its ranks, American isolationists had done everything they could to impede Roosevelt's attempts to help Britain—and even to rearm the United States. Late in the autumn of 1941—just a few weeks before war came— the Draft Act, upon which depended the continued existence of the new American armies, was continued for one additional year by a majority of one single vote in Congress! Furthermore, enraged by the surprise Japanese attack on Pearl Harbor on December 7, 1941, many Americans thought their country should devote itself to winning the war in the Pacific without taking on additional enemies in Europe. If Hitler had not declared war against the United States when he did, it is problematical whether Roosevelt would have been able to lead a united America into war against Germany.

Although Der Fuehrer, in common with many of his generals, held American military power in contempt, he had been wise enough during the first two years of war to do everything in his power to keep the United States neutral. For this purpose large sums of money were spent by the German Embassy in Washington to pay newspaper writers, support the America-First Committee, and even to bribe congressmen. And in the early days of the war German submarines were instructed not to attack American merchant vessels. Even later, when the U. S. Navy had taken over some of the British Fleet's convoy duties in safeguarding the tremendous American Lend-Lease shipment of arms and munitions to England, German U-boats were ordered to avoid incidents with American naval vessels.

Not that Hitler did not intend to strike down the United States as soon as he could. On many occasions he spoke of how he would "severely punish" the upstart Americans, a "degenerate and mongreloid race without culture or tradition," for daring to aid his British enemies. But Hitler wanted to finish off Britain first. Then there would be time to attack America. It was largely to keep the United States out of the war that Der Fuehrer had signed the Tripartite Pact with Italy and Japan. It was assumed that the United States would not risk war in Europe with the Japanese threatening war in the Pacific. Japan was to be a makeweight against American intervention in the European war.

But by March 26, 1941, with German troops about to attack the Balkan nations and with the war against Russia looming ahead, Hitler had changed his mind. One of the principal reasons for his onslaught on the Soviet Union was to crush her and thereby make the

British realize that they could never hope for Russian intervention to win the war. But, aside from the Soviet Union, Britain also had hopes of eventual American intervention. Therefore the United States must also be crushed. On the afternoon of March 26, Hitler told Yosuke Matsuoka, the Japanese Foreign Minister, who was visiting Berlin: "Never in the human imagination could there be a better moment for Japan to strike in the Pacific than now." The Japanese Fleet would easily defeat the U.S. Navy and, with British forces tied up in Europe and America not yet rearmed, the way would be open for a Japanese conquest of all of East Asia. Hitler, of course, hoped to embroil Japan in a war against the United States which would prevent further American aid to England and forestall American aid to Russia. But on April 4, Der Fuehrer went even further. He solemnly promised that if Japan should go to war with the United States, Germany would join her. "Germany has made her preparations so that no American soldier could land in Europe," Hitler boasted. Germany would wage a vigorous war against America with U-boats and the Luftwaffe, and would be more than a match for America, entirely apart from the fact that German soldiers were, obviously, far superior to Americans.

But the Japanese needed no German urging to attack the United States. They had their own reasons and their own policies to follow. Therefore the sudden Japanese attack on the U.S. Fleet at Pearl Harbor came as a complete surprise to Germany as it did to the United States. But Hitler's hesitation of four days before fulfilling his promise to the Japanese was not based on considerations of international strategy, but only on how to make war against America palatable to the German people, who remembered only too well the result of their previous war with the United States. Der Fuehrer himself had no fears. Later he said: "I don't see much future for the Americans. It's a decayed country. And they have their racial problems, and the problem of social inequalities. My feelings against Americanism are feelings of hatred and deep repugnance. How can one expect a state like that to hold together—a country where everything is built on the dollar?"

And so, on December 11, 1941, before a cheering mob of Reichstag deputies, Hitler, after reciting hours of lies and insults about America, led his country into war against the United States. The German General Staff may have shuddered, the German people may have worried, but Hitler and his cronies were overjoyed at the prospect of fighting another 135 million people and the largest industrial establishment on earth! Thus, as 1941 drew to its close, the mighty German war machine had suffered a serious reversal in Russia, had failed to conquer the indomitable British, and was now faced with a worldwide coalition against it. But it was by no means defeated yet.

As the Russian counteroffensive ran out of steam at the beginning of March 1942, then stopped altogether with the coming of the heavy spring rains, Hitler planned a series of massive blows against his enemies. While they were not so ambitious as his plans of the previous year, they were large enough. His aim was to seize the Russian oilfields in the Caucasus. If that could be accomplished, then Russia's war machine would fall to pieces. The city of Stalingrad, on the bend of the Volga River above the Caucasus, became the prime objective of the planned German offensive. But the terrible winter campaign of 1941 had cost the German Army over a million casualties. Among 12 armored divisions only 140 serviceable tanks could be gathered. It would require a speedy and mighty effort by German industry to replace the mechanized and armored equipment needed for a new offensive. And it would require more men, hundreds of thousands of them, to fill out the thinned German ranks. Since German manpower was already being used to its utmost both in the Army and in industry, Hitler turned to his allies for men. Thirteen Hungarian, 27 Romanian, 9 Italian, 2 Slovak, and 1 Spanish division were hastily recruited. Although these 52 Allied divisions represented one quarter of all the German forces fighting in Russia, the German generals were worried about their fighting qualities. In this they were correct, as future operations were to prove.

But before the great German offensive in Russia started, German troops in Africa won a startling victory. There General Erwin Rommel's famed Afrika Korps (which had been reinforced to two armored divisions and a motorized infantry division), in cooperation with eight Italian divisions, struck the British Desert Army on May 27, 1942. In a series of lightning thrusts and savage tank battles the Germans quickly drove the British back to the Egyptian village of El Alamein, which was only sixty-five miles from the Suez Canal. Now, with even modest reinforcements and fresh supplies, Rommel could easily brush aside the remnants of the British forces, capture Suez, conquer the Middle East, and perhaps even swing north to join German forces pushing down through the Caucasus. But Hitler, as we have seen, never understood the possibilities of global warfare. In spite of making General Rommel a field marshal and showering him with congratulations, Der Fuehrer did nothing to reinforce the Afrika Korps. That, he thought, could wait until after the success of the Russian offensive. Thus, although the German Army in Africa reached El Alamein on the crest of victory, they arrived there with only 125 tanks still operational. And, although the Pyramids were almost in sight, they could go no farther. This was especially disappointing to Mussolini because the vain Italian dictator was waiting behind the German lines to lead the triumphal parade into Cairo.

Meanwhile the huge German offensive in southern Russia had been launched with great success. Although Russian resistance was as stubborn as ever, German armies pushed forward steadily until, on August 23, 1942, they reached the Volga River north of Stalingrad. The vital Maikop oilfields had already been captured (the Russians destroyed them before retreating) and the remaining Russian fields in the Caucasus were only fifty miles beyond German advance units. The German objectives, it seemed, were attained.

But as Der Fuehrer's divisions advanced to the Volga, their objective—at least as far as Hitler was concerned—subtly changed. Originally they had intended to cut off Russian oil; and this they were now in a position to do. But, perhaps because it bore the name of the Soviet leader, the city of Stalingrad began to assume more and more importance in Hitler's mind. The German Sixth Army, under the command of General Friedrich von Paulus, had been assigned the task of capturing Stalingrad and by the middle of September was fighting in the outskirts of that city. The struggle became bitter as the Russians defended every house and basement, every street and alley, of the demolished city. Hitler, however, kept throwing in fresh divisions; he was determined to conquer Stalingrad at any price. In vain his General Staff pointed out to him the long, exposed, and thinly held German flank above the beleaguered city. Hitler was convinced that once again—and this time definitively—the Russian armies were destroyed. When a staff officer read aloud a report which showed that more than a million Russian troops were massing on the exposed German flank, and that Russian tank production amounted to at least 1,200 tanks per month, Hitler attacked the officer with clenched fists and foaming lips.

And while German troops stood at the threshold of Suez and astride the Russian oil lifelines, what of the war in the West? The American armies were not yet trained, the British forces not yet fully equipped. And German U-boats were sinking more than 700,000 tons of Allied shipping per month in the Atlantic. While the RAF continued to bomb German cities, these attacks were thus far only of nuisance value to the Allies. Although the first small contingents of American troops had arrived in Great Britain, there was no possibility at all that the Allies would attempt even a small invasion of Europe in 1942. Hitler had made some extreme military gambles that year—and it appeared that he was going to win them.

The first indication that the time of German victories was at an end came in Egypt. There the Afrika Korps and its Italian allies launched a final assault against the British positions at El Alamein on August 31, 1942. The battle raged back and forth for three days until finally Field Marshal Rommel realized he would not break through the British lines, and retired to go over to the defensive. He had come up against a British Army which had been completely re-equipped and was now under the command of an imaginative and fiery leader—General Sir Bernard Law Montgomery. What a properly equipped and ably led British Army could do against the German "supermen" was now demonstrated. On October 23, 1942, at 9:40 P.M., under cover of a tremendous artillery barrage, General Montgomery launched his Army on a savage attack against the German lines. After a week of bitter fighting, British troops broke through and began to roll up the Italian divisions on Rommel's southern flank. By the evening of November 4 the Germans were fleeing from as complete a defeat as any German Army had ever suffered. In fighting at El Alamein, Field Marshal Rommel lost over half of his Army killed, wounded, or captured, all his remaining tanks and most of his heavy weapons and transport. Within two weeks the victorious British Desert Army had advanced more than 700 miles—and Rommel was still running!

Then, on November 8, Anglo-American troops under the command of General Dwight Eisenhower landed at several places on the French North African coast. Under convoy by a mighty naval armada, the troopships which had come from England and from across the Atlantic began pouring a large Allied Army ashore in the face of light French opposition, which soon turned into cooperation. This blow came as a complete surprise to Hitler, if not to his worried General Staff. Now Rommel's armies would be taken in the rear and all of North Africa transformed into a giant Allied staging area for a possible assault against Italy. Hitler could think of nothing better to do than to rush German reinforcements into Tunisia in North Africa just a few days before Anglo-American forces would have reached there. These reinforcements, which were to reach the number of 240,000 men, were, of course, cut off from all hope of supply by Allied control of the Mediterranean. Before too many months had passed, they would all be marching into Allied prisoner-of-war camps.

But if the news from Africa was bad, the news which now came from the Russian front was catastrophic. For there, in the teeth of a raging blizzard on November 19, thirteen Russian armies, equipped with thousands of tanks, had attacked that long, exposed German flank north of Stalingrad. They quickly broke through the Romanian and Hungarian forces in this area and raced south to link up with other Russian armies which were attacking south of Stalingrad. If General von Paulus' Sixth Army was not to be surrounded it would have to retreat immediately. But when this was suggested by his generals, Hitler flew into one of his rages, screaming: "I won't leave the Volga! I won't go back from the Volga!" Orders were issued to General von Paulus that he must hold Stalingrad at all costs. Retreat was absolutely forbidden. The order was a death sentence to the 200,000 men of the German Sixth Army.

By November 22 the Russians had cut off Stalingrad from the rest of the German Army—and that army was now fleeing back from the Caucasus and from the banks of the Volga, reeling under the blows of the Soviet offensive. An attempt to break through the Russian ring of steel around the city was decisively beaten on December 22, 1942. The German Army in Stalingrad was doomed.

On January 8, 1943, the Red Army command at Stalingrad offered the Germans a chance to surrender. But when General von Paulus radioed for permission to do so, his request was curtly refused. Therefore, on January 10, following a barrage by 5,000 guns, the Russians commenced their final assault on the city. The fighting was bitter and bloody, but after six days the German forces had been battered into a corner. Once again, on January 24, the Russians gave their enemies an opportunity to surrender. General von Paulus radioed to Hitler: "Troops without ammunition or food . . . 18,000 wounded without any supplies or dressings or drugs . . . further defense senseless . . ."

Hitler replied: "Surrender is forbidden. Sixth Army will hold their positions to the last man and the last round . . ."

On January 30, Paulus radioed that collapse could not be postponed more than twenty-four hours. Hitler's reaction was to make General von Paulus a field marshal, because, as he remarked, there was no record in military history of a German field marshal being taken prisoner. But there is a first time for everything. The next day Field Marshal von Paulus surrendered to the Russians and, a few days later, isolated German units still holding out in the rest of Stalingrad were overrun by Soviet forces. By February 2 the long and bloody Battle of Stalingrad was over: 91,000 German soldiers and 24 generals were marched out of the ice-covered ruins of the once-great city as prisoners of war. Behind them they left over 200,000 German dead and all hope of eventual German victory in the war. Hitler did well to proclaim four days of national mourning throughout Germany.

Every spring since 1940 had brought great German offensives in Europe. The peoples of that unhappy continent had cowered in terror, wondering where the mighty German war machine would strike next. But the spring of 1943 was to be different. Now it was the turn of the Allies and of the Russians to dictate where and when and how battles would be fought. Germany had lost the initiative in the war, and it now passed irrevocably into the hands of the people against whom Hitler had launched his wars of conquest. A day of wrath and judgment was approaching for Germany, and no amount of wishful thinking could postpone it.

A foretaste of what was in store for the Third Reich was the downfall of Mussolini and the collapse of Fascist Italy. By early May of 1943 the Allied armies in North Africa had finished mopping up the last German-Italian forces in Tunisia. Obviously their next objective would be Sicily and/or the Italian mainland. The nightmare which had kept Mussolini out of the war until he'd thought it won had now become grim reality. And to oppose Eisenhower's victorious Anglo-American armies, fleets, and air forces Italy could muster only demoralized, badly equipped troops and a population sick of war. Already strikes had broken out in the industrial cities of Milan and Turin in the north, with marching workers demanding peace.

On July 10 the Allied armies landed in Sicily. Italian divisions facing them simply collapsed while the island's population (including the dreaded all-powerful

Mafia) generally cooperated with troops who appeared to them as liberators rather than enemies. In an attempt to stiffen Mussolini's nerves Hitler summoned the Italian dictator to Feltre in northern Italy for a meeting on July 19. Once again he put on a show of confidence for his faltering friend, once again the Nazi leader erupted in a flow of verbal theatrics which lasted for hours. But Mussolini was so depressed by now that he could barely understand the endless tirade of words poured upon him. And, to cap matters, news arrived that the first heavy Allied air raid had struck Rome.

When Mussolini, a tired and broken man, returned to Rome, he found himself faced with a revolt by his own Fascist party followers. And on the evening of July 25 the Italian dictator was summoned to a conference with King Victor Emmanuel. Mussolini was utterly unprepared for what followed. First the King told him that Italy had gone to pieces, that the soldiers would no longer fight, that he (Mussolini) was the most hated man in Italy. Then the King summoned waiting policemen, had Mussolini arrested like any ordinary criminal and carted off to jail in an ambulance! Such was the downfall of Hitler's ally, the arrogant and boastful dictator who had brought death and misery to so many victims in Spain, Albania, Ethiopia, and Greece—and to his own Italian people. The measure of his disgrace may be seen in the fact that not a shot was fired, nor a voice raised in his defense; on the contrary, Italians everywhere rejoiced in his humiliation.

Marshal Pietro Badoglio, who had headed the plot to remove Mussolini, now formed an interim government and set out immediately to make peace with the Allies.

Hitler's reaction to the news of his friend's downfall was one of deep shock and bitter rage. But this did not prevent him from laying plans to save what he could of the German position in Italy. His first thought was for vengeance on those who had overthrown his friend. He ordered his generals to prepare plans for a German armored division stationed near Rome to drive into the city and arrest Badoglio, the King, and all the other members of the new government. When someone pointed out that these men might take refuge in the Vatican, Hitler exploded: "I'll go right into the Vatican. Do you think the Vatican embarrasses me? We'll take that over right away. . . . The entire diplomatic corps are in there. . . . That rabble. . . . We'll get that bunch of swine out of there!"

On a more practical level, Hitler issued orders that the Alpine passes between Italy and Germany be secured by German troops, and began rushing divisions to strengthen Field Marshal Albert Kesselring's German forces, which were opposing the advance of Allied troops up the Italian peninsula and which now had to worry that they might be attacked by Italian troops in their rear. Plans were made to rescue Mussolini, seize Rome, and reinstall a Fascist regime into power and to seize all of Italy, disarming Italian troops and capturing the Italian Fleet. Upon the announcement (on September 8, 1943) that Italy had concluded an armistice with the Allies, these German plans were put into operation. The delay in Eisenhower's advance on Rome gave the energetic Kesselring a chance to carry out his instructions to disarm Italian troops, seize control of the country, and establish a heavily fortified line against the Allies just north of Naples. To Hitler's rage, however, both the Italian government (including the King) and the Italian Fleet escaped his clutches, fleeing to the Allies.

The part of the German plan which called for the rescue of Mussolini had to wait until the Germans could find out where he was being held. But by early

September 1943, Der Fuehrer learned that his friend was being held atop one of the highest peaks in the Apennine Mountains in southern Italy. Under the leadership of an Austrian SS officer and roughneck named Otto Skorzeny, a specially trained force of German airborne troops landed in gliders around the hotel on September 13. With them they had brought a captive Italian general who was marched ahead of them while Skorzeny cried out: "Don't fire on an Italian general!" It was hardly necessary, for at the first appearance of the German troops the police who had been guarding Mussolini (who watched the proceedings from a second-story window of the hotel) took to the hills. In minutes Mussolini had been bundled into a small plane, which flew him to Rome, and from there was transported in a Luftwaffe plane to Vienna. The German rescue of the former Italian dictator was certainly one of the most daring feats of the entire war, but it had little effect on its course.

If 1943 brought disaster to Italy, it also brought catastrophe to the German armies in Russia. On July 5, 1943, Hitler had launched what was to prove his last offensive against the Soviet Union. On that day half a million German troops, supported by 17 armored divisions which had been re-equipped with the new heavy Tiger tanks, threw themselves against the Russian positions around the city of Kursk. But the Russians had been prepared for this blow and had massed their own tank forces. In the greatest tank action ever fought thousands of Russian and German tanks collided in a battle which lasted for more than two weeks. By July 22 the newspapers in Moscow were joyously proclaiming in banner headlines: "The Tigers Are Burning!" And so they were. By that date the Germans had lost over half of all their tanks and begun to retreat. At the same time huge Russian armies on other fronts began their first summer offensive of the war—an offensive which was to carry them to Berlin. All summer long the Russians advanced. And the Russian cities which had fallen to the Nazis in the early days of the war now began to appear once again in the headlines—recaptured by Soviet armies. Nowhere could the shattered German armies form a strong line of resistance. By the end of 1943 Russian forces were approaching the borders of Poland, Romania, and Czechoslovakia.

The year 1943 also saw a turning point in the Battle of the Atlantic. Using new techniques of air-sea cooperation, and employing new radar search devices, the Allies slowly but surely began to get the upper hand over the dreaded U-boats. The German Navy was now under the command of Admiral Karl Doenitz, a U-boat specialist who had replaced Admiral Raeder on January 30, 1943, when that officer fell from Hitler's graces. Doenitz could do nothing to halt the mounting destruction of his undersea forces. By May of 1943 the Allies were sinking German U-boats at a fearful rate (37 in May alone) and Doenitz withdrew his submarines from Atlantic waters. When they again appeared, in the autumn of 1943, the Allies were able to sink one U-boat for every freighter sunk—a rate of loss which spelled total victory over the once mighty German submarine fleet. And over the now secure waters of the Atlantic a vast tide of arms and men was pouring into Britain from America. The great Allied buildup for "Operation Overlord"—the invasion of Western Europe—had commenced, and there was nothing Hitler could do to halt or even delay it.

But if these disasters in distant Russia and Italy and on the Atlantic worried the German people, the meaning of the terrible war they had started was really brought home to them by the increasing Allied air attacks on German cities. The RAF by night and the American Eighth Air Force by day ranged at will deep into German territory, raining fire and destruction on

German homes and factories. Now the terror which Germans had inflicted on the defenseless inhabitants of Rotterdam and Warsaw and Belgrade and Coventry and London was being repaid a thousandfold. Clouds of a thousand heavy bombers at a time darkened the skies of Dortmund, Essen, Cologne, Hamburg, Berlin —and scores of other German cities and towns. Hundreds of thousands of Germans now learned how it felt to be made homeless overnight, to see their places of work blown to bits, to cower in air-raid shelters night after night and day after day while thousands of tons of high explosives rained down overhead.

And, although the German people bore these afflictions as bravely as the British had during the Luftwaffe's terror bombing of London, their morale was undermined by the constant flow of bad news from all fronts and a growing realization that they were alone, the objects of the hatred of most of mankind, who viewed their destruction as retribution for unspeakable crimes. As 1943 turned into 1944, Germans came to realize that the future no longer existed for them.

Hitler and his followers were, of course, determined to resist to the bitter end. But even among the top Nazis the impossibility of Germany's position was now becoming painfully evident. Soon the Allied invasion of Western Europe would commence—and that would spell the end, because Germany could certainly not fight a two-front war. It was even problematical if Germany could defend herself against the oncoming Russians.

It was during the winter of 1943-44 that Hitler, Goebbels, Goering, and the German generals began to wonder if there was not some way they could make peace with either Russia or the Allies and continue the war on only a single front. To make peace with Stalin was a very remote possibility. Too many crimes had been committed by the Germans in Russia. Besides, there still remained that ancient German urge to conquer the east for "living space." But perhaps peace might be made with the Western Allies. Perhaps they would once again fall for that old Nazi bogey, the "Bolshevik menace." If Germany could paint herself as the defender of "Western civilization" against the onrushing "Communist hordes," perhaps the Allies would even help her to fight against Russia.

Josef Goebbels, Hitler's twisted propaganda chief, was now entering such thoughts in his personal diary. "The English," he wrote, "don't want a Bolshevik Europe under any circumstances . . . they will no doubt show an inclination toward a compromise with us . . . Churchill himself is an old anti-Bolshevik . . ."

But this was only whistling in the dark. Churchill and Roosevelt had already proclaimed their intention of accepting only "unconditional surrender" from Germany and their determination not to desert their Russian ally under any circumstances. Nor was it in any way conceivable that either Churchill or Roosevelt would have entered into any kind of negotiations with the bloodstained and maniacal leadership of the Third Reich. If Germany was to have peace before she was utterly destroyed, it could only be on the basis of total surrender, and that surrender, if it came, could only be offered by a German government which had nothing to do with nazism. In other words, if the Germans wanted to save themselves from the final calamity, they would themselves have to act against Hitler and his henchmen first.

The fact that there were Germans prepared to act against Hitler—prepared to give their lives if need be to erase the foul Nazi dictatorship which had for so long disgraced their nation—must not be forgotten. Although their number was pitifully few, their plans often vague, and their activities hampered by indecisiveness, their personal courage was indisputable. The example of their conduct cast a bright, if tiny, ray of light from the darkness into which the German character had plunged. And by the spring of 1944 these men were ready to strike.

Ten

THE TWILIGHT OF THE GODS

GENERAL LUDWIG BECK, SINCE THE DAY HE HAD RE-
signed as Chief of the General Staff in protest against
Hitler's plans to annex Czechoslovakia, had not ceased
to oppose nazism. Over the years he had concentrated
on trying to win the support of high-ranking Army officers for various plots to arrest or kill Der Fuehrer,
and gradually had succeeded in building up wide con-
tacts and a loosely knit conspiracy of those who
thought as he did. Political spark plug of Beck's following was Carl Goerdeler, the former mayor of Leipzig, while one of the most energetic (and clear thinking) of his followers was General Henning von Tresckow, Chief of Staff of Army Group Center in Russia.
Ulrich von Hassell, former German ambassador to
Italy, lent diplomatic advice. Many other German
Army officers of high and low rank were part of Beck's
conspiracy. Admiral Wilhelm Canaris lent the wide resources of his Army Intelligence Service to the plot
and Count Wolff von Helldorff, Chief of the Berlin Police, stood ready to aid the conspiracy.

The Beck group was conservative in its hopes for
the future. They envisaged a democratic but conserva-

tive Germany, ruled possibly by one of the Hohenzollern heirs through a constitutional monarchy on the English style. They hoped to conclude an armistice with the Western Allies after wiping out the Hitler regime—but to continue resistance against the Russians.

Early in March 1943, General von Tresckow and one of his junior officers, Fabian von Schlabrendorff (both of the Beck group), decided the time had come to act. Through Admiral Canaris' Intelligence Service they secured a British-made time bomb (a silent and more efficient device than time bombs of German manufacture). The principle on which the bomb worked was simple: when a button was pressed, a small bottle inside was broken, which in turn released a corrosive acid which ate away a wire which held back a spring which released the detonator. By using heavier or thinner wire, the time of the explosion could be more or less controlled in advance. Schlabrendorff was able to place one of these bombs, disguised as a bottle of brandy, aboard Hitler's plane on March 13 as it took off from Smolensk on a flight back to Der Fuehrer's headquarters in East Prussia. But, although by great good luck the bomb was never discovered, it failed to explode. It had worked—but the detonator had not fired.

On March 21, 1943, another attempt was made on Hitler's life. This one was to be a suicide mission. Colonel Freiherr von Gersdorff, Chief of Intelligence of Army Group Center, volunteered to place two of the British bombs in his overcoat pocket. Then, as Hitler passed him during an inspection of Russian war trophies in Berlin, the brave colonel was to set the fuses, grab Der Fuehrer and blow them both to smithereens. The plan failed because Hitler changed his schedule at the last moment. Several further attempts against the Nazi dictator were also frustrated.

One of these unsuccessful attempts was made by Lieutenant Colonel Klaus Philipp Schenk, Count von

Stauffenberg, a man who because of his dedication, sense of mission, efficiency, and brilliance now became the active leader of the anti-Hitler conspirators.

Count von Stauffenberg had been born in 1907, of an old, aristocratic, and devoutly Catholic South German family. His education was excellent and his performance at the War Academy in Berlin from 1936 to 1938 attracted favorable attention from the Army High Command. But by this time von Stauffenberg was an anti-Nazi. Apparently it was the anti-Jewish pogrom of that year which finally decided him. He served with distinction in Poland, France, and Russia, his anti-Nazi feelings growing steadily stronger as he saw the misery Hitler brought to conquered countries. On April 7, 1943, while on duty in Tunisia, von Stauffenberg's car ran over a land mine. The count lost his left eye, his right hand and two fingers of his left hand. For several weeks in the Munich hospital it seemed that Stauffenberg would be totally blind. But his sight in one eye was saved. Later, when he was convalescing at his home, he told his wife, the Countess Nina (they had four children), that he felt he had to do something to save Germany, that all General Staff officers had to shoulder their share of the responsibility.

By October of 1943, Stauffenberg was back in Berlin working at the Army Office—and practicing with a pair of tongs how to set off one of Canaris' British time bombs.

In February 1944 the conspirators received a tremendous and unexpected reinforcement. Field Marshal Erwin Rommel, the "desert fox" and the most popular of all Germany's commanders, joined the Beck group. Rommel, since his defeat in Africa, had been named commander of the German Army in France, with orders to defend Hitler's "Fortress Europe" against the expected Allied invasion. Disgusted by Hitler's mismanagement of the war and now deeply opposed to the Nazi regime on moral grounds, Rommel planned to arrest all SS and Gestapo men in France, conclude an immediate armistice with the Allies, withdraw to Germany, and use his forces to support a new government which would be headed by the underground resistance leaders. He planned to do this, that is, provided Stauffenberg's plan to kill Hitler and seize control of Berlin worked.

Stauffenberg's plans for Berlin depended upon speed. The large SS and Gestapo units, Goering's antiaircraft personnel, government ministers—all would have to be arrested within two hours of Hitler's death. Furthermore, the Berlin radio station and other key communications points would have to be seized. Forces for these tasks were to be drawn from the Berlin units of the Home Army (overage or underage conscripts unfit for the regular Army) and by Count Helldorff's Berlin Police. By June of 1944 the plans were ripe.

Then suddenly—it came as a complete tactical surprise to the German High Command—transported in more than a thousand ships, convoyed by tremendous fleets, under cover of an air umbrella of 17,000 planes, the Anglo-American armies under the command of Eisenhower and Montgomery landed on June 6, 1944, in Normandy. Within days this mighty invasion force had secured the entire Normandy peninsula. Over the next month thousands of tons of supplies poured ashore and hundreds of thousands of men. Soon the battered and demoralized German forces in France would be unable to hold this tremendous Allied Army in Normandy. Furthermore, the Russians had mounted a new offensive. By July 4, 1944, the German forces had been smashed, and Red Army troops crossed the Polish border and drove on East Prussia. When all available reserves were thrown in to protect this first bit of Germany to come under enemy fire, the western armies were weakened. All during the second half of July, British and American forces fought to break out of the Normandy peninsula—and ground up German divisions by the score.

Rommel had pleaded insistently with Hitler to find some way of ending the war before Germany was invaded from both east and west. By July 15, Rommel knew that Der Fuehrer would never surrender and that only his death would solve the problem. But on July 17, as he was driving back to his front-line headquarters, Rommel's car was strafed by low-flying Allied fighter planes. Rommel was severely wounded and was lost—temporarily at least—to the conspiracy. This was a heavy blow to Beck and Stauffenberg. But they determined to proceed anyhow. As General von Tresckow said: "The assassination must be attempted at any cost. Even should it fail, the attempt to seize power in the capital must be undertaken. We must prove to the world and to future generations that the men of the German Resistance Movement dared to take the decisive step and to hazard their lives upon it. Compared with this object, nothing else matters."

Shortly after 10 A.M. on the morning of July 20, 1944, Colonel von Stauffenberg arrived at Hitler's headquarters—the "wolf's lair" in East Prussia. He had been summoned to report on the state of the Home Army. But in his briefcase, along with papers and reports, Stauffenberg carried one of the British time bombs. At a few minutes before 12:30, Stauffenberg pressed the button on his bomb and then carried it into Hitler's conference room as he was called to make his report. He now had ten minutes before the bomb would explode. Calmly he greeted Hitler, took a seat at the large conference table—and placed his briefcase on the floor beside Der Fuehrer's chair. Four minutes had gone by. While staff officers discussed the day's bad news from the Russian front for Hitler's benefit, Stauffenberg stole from the room. Five minutes to go. As Hitler and his aides bent over military maps, Stauffenberg made his way out of the conference building and over to the office of General Erich Fellgiebel. Fellgiebel was in on the conspiracy. As Signals Chief of the Fuehrer's headquarters, it would be his job to cut all communications with the outside world once the bomb had done its work.

12:42 P.M.—a tremendous explosion tore the Fuehrer's conference building to pieces. Bodies came flying out through shattered windows, debris fell over a wide area, smoke billowed high into the sky. Stauffenberg and Fellgiebel had not the slightest doubt that everyone—including Hitler—who had been inside that conference building was now dead. Stauffenberg hurried away to catch his plane back to Berlin. Fellgiebel, according to plan, now, cut all communications with the outside world. To get out of the headquarters area Stauffenberg bluffed and blustered his way past three separate guard points. By 1 P.M. he was airborne for Berlin. Fellgiebel had already telephoned the conspirators in Berlin that Hitler had been killed. Stauffenberg could only wait out the next three hours as his plane sped to Berlin and hope that things had gone well in the capital.

But in Berlin things hardly went at all. The high-ranking Army officers who were to have acted so decisively and, above all, *speedily,* displayed a strange dilatoriness. Under the leadership of General Beck they had seized control of the War Ministry, but, as Stauffenberg discovered when he arrived there at 4:10 P.M., they had not issued orders to seize the Berlin Radio, they had not done anything to seal off the SS and Gestapo units, nor had they arrested Goebbels and other government ministers in Berlin. They had, in fact, gone far enough to ensure their own executions for high treason but not far enough to win.

The basic reason for this, as Stauffenberg learned to his complete amazement, was that Hitler had not been killed. The bomb, which had burst only feet from Der Fuehrer and killed and wounded many others in the conference room, had only stunned Hitler, punctured his cardrums, and badly bruised his right arm. The tiny fact that had saved his life was simply that after Stauffenberg had left the conference table, another officer had moved the briefcase a few feet—to a place behind one of the heavy oak table supports. When the blast occurred, Hitler was protected from its full impact by the table support and the table itself. Furthermore, when General Fellgiebel had telephoned to Berlin, he had to report that Hitler was still alive. This had taken the heart out of some of the higher-ranking Army officers whose cooperation depended upon Hitler's death.

Despite the energy with which Stauffenberg now threw himself into the task of making the conspiracy work even though Hitler was not dead, the plot was doomed. Goebbels, who had been in Berlin all day without being aware that an anti-Nazi uprising was supposed to be going on, was finally alerted when a junior officer and a few men dispatched by Stauffenberg arrived to arrest him. But the wily Propaganda Minister had little difficulty in talking the officer out of it. Finally he put through a call to Hitler's headquarters in East Prussia (communications had been restored by then) and received instructions to crush the Berlin conspirators immediately. By this time SS units (and officers who had been in on the conspiracy but were now frightened and determined to prove their loyalty to Der Fuehrer) had started to act on their own.

At 9 P.M. Stauffenberg and his men at the War Ministry heard, to their horror and amazement, that Hitler would himself address the German nation later that same night over the radio. By 10:30 Nazi officers had

retaken control of the War Ministry and arrested
Stauffenberg, Beck, and the others. These officers were
under the command of General Friedrich Fromm,
Commander of the Home Army. General Fromm had
been in on the conspiracy for a long time but had refused to act when it became clear that Hitler was not
dead. Now he was in a hurry to cover up his tracks.
Shortly after midnight on July 21 the rebel officers
were machine-gunned in the courtyard of the War
Ministry. As he died Stauffenberg cried: "Long live
Free Germany!"

Hitler's vengeance was terrible. Practically all of the
conspirators were found out, put to dreadful torture at
the hands of the Gestapo, their friends and relatives
carted off to concentration camps, and they themselves
brought up for mock trials before the People's Court,
where they were reviled and shouted down. Over
5,000 conspirators were killed—most of them by
strangling with piano wire. Some, like General Fromm,
found that their betrayal of the conspiracy could not
save them; they were executed anyhow. Field Marshal
Rommel was forced to take poison on pain of having
his family placed in a concentration camp. Practically
all the men who had led the anti-Hitler plot were destroyed: General Ludwig Beck, Admiral Wilhelm Canaris, Ulrich von Hassell, Carl Goerdeler—all met a
barbarous end at the hands of Himmler's SS and Gestapo. But their epitaph was pronounced by General
Tresckow, who, just before he killed himself on July
21, said: ". . . my conviction remains unshaken—we
have done the right thing. Hitler is not only the archenemy of Germany: he is the archenemy of the world. In
a few hours I shall stand before God, answering for my
actions and for my omissions. I think I shall be able to
uphold with a clear conscience all that I have done in
the fight against Hitler . . . the worth of a man is certain only if he is prepared to sacrifice his life for his

convictions." Of the worth of the men who gave their lives trying to kill Hitler there can be no doubt. If the world cannot forget the terrible German barbarism of the Nazi era, it should also remember the courage and idealism and sacrifice of those Germans who paid their debt to humanity with their lives.

And long before the last of the conspirators was strangled, like the wrath of God the war came home to Germany. Within a matter of weeks, during the summer of 1944, the Americans and British had smashed the German armies in the west and liberated France and Belgium. Now they prepared to plunge into Germany itself. In the east, Russian forces were approaching the German borders through Poland and from the southeast through Yugoslavia, Hungary, and Czechoslovakia. Never, since the time of Napoleon, had German troops had to fight on German soil. But now the fire and destruction Germany had loosed against the world was to return to its starting place with greater fury.

Hitler, his mind showing greater and greater signs of decay, still clung to the hope of a division between his enemies. On August 31, 1944, he told his generals: "The time will come when the tension between the Allies will become so great that the break will occur. All the coalitions in history have disintegrated sooner or later."

With absolute disaster looming, Goebbels was ordered to take charge of "total mobilization," and Heinrich Himmler undertook to raise *Volks* (People's) divisions for the defense of the Fatherland. Boys as young as fifteen and men as old as sixty were now drafted. Schools, universities, and factories were combed and combed again for men. Furthermore, drastic action was taken to stop the swelling flow of desertions from the Army. On September 10, Himmler decreed that the families of deserters would be shot.

Special flying squads of SS thugs were organized to round up deserters or stragglers, try them summarily, and hang them. The sight of German soldiers hanging from lampposts with crudely lettered signs reading "I deserted" pinned to their lifeless bodies was often one of the first to greet the eyes of Anglo-American troops as they entered German towns.

But Hitler still had one daring surprise to spring on the victorious Allied armies. All through the autumn of 1944 he had scraped the bottom of Germany's manpower barrel and declining industrial output. Denuding other fronts of troops and equipment, by December he had gathered together 28 divisions, including 9 armored divisions equipped with 2,500 tanks and self-propelled guns. This formidable force was thrown against a weakly held section of the American lines in the Ardennes on December 16, 1944. Hitler's plan, which was far beyond his means, was to punch a hole in the Allied line and then swing north to capture Antwerp and thereby cut off the Anglo-American armies in Belgium and Holland. It was a smaller-scale version of the successful offensive against the French in 1940. But it was carried out with far smaller forces and it was opposed by an entirely different sort of enemy. At first, due to the surprise and to the fact that fog prevented Allied air power from intervening, the Germans had some success. But their advance was held up by the stubborn resistance of the U.S. 101st Airborne Division, whose commander, General Anthony C. McAuliffe, replied to a German demand that he surrender with the single word: "Nuts!" By December 22 the German offensive was stalled. The next day the skies cleared and swarms of Allied planes rose to attack the German supply lines and massed tank formations. Already British and American armored divisions were pushing to cut off the German forces, and by January 16 the Germans had been routed. The Battle of the

Bulge gained nothing for Hitler, but it used up his last effective reserves of arms and men.

Before the German Ardennes offensive Hitler had been warned by his generals that the Russians were massing for a great offensive in the east. They begged him not to throw away Germany's last forces on a gamble in the west but to preserve them to try to hold the Russians. But Hitler flew into a rage and raved about this being the "greatest bluff since Genghis Khan!" He ought to have remembered that Genghis Khan never bluffed about anything.

On January 12, 1945, over 300 Russian divisions resumed the offensive on all fronts. The violent Soviet attack, backed by thousands of tanks, broke like a tidal wave over the thin German forces in Poland, East Prussia, and the Balkans. By January 27, Russian forces had advanced 220 miles, cutting off both East and West Prussia and Silesia from the Fatherland. Soviet armies were now less than a hundred miles from Berlin.

It was from the Chancellery building (and, due to incessant Allied air attack, the huge underground bunker beneath it) that Hitler continued to direct his war after January 1945. He was never to leave it. Der Fuehrer had by this time been reduced to a physical wreck. The maniacal fervor with which he misdirected his armies, the paranoid suspicions which clouded his mind with every new German defeat, the unhealthy life in underground bunkers where he had spent most of the past few years—and the constant flow of drugs which Dr. Morell continued to administer—had completely undermined his health. Visitors described him as gray, pallid, with an uncurable shakiness in his hands, and with a strange, devilish flicker in his clouded eyes.

By the middle of March, Eisenhower's armies had almost surrounded Germany's industrial Ruhr, destroying large German forces in the process, and had crossed the Rhine in strength. Hitler's reaction was to issue a general order requiring that all military, industrial, communications, and transportation installations, as well as all stocks of food, fuel, and other materials all over Germany be destroyed to keep them from falling into enemy hands. By the terms of this order Germany would have turned into one vast wasteland. After the war the German people would have starved by the millions. But Hitler no longer cared for the fate of the German people. When Albert Speer, the energetic Economic Coordinator of Germany's war economy, protested that this order was a death sentence for the German population, Der Fuehrer replied: "If the war is lost, the nation will also perish . . . this nation will have proved to be the weaker one. . . . Besides, those who remain after the battle are only the inferior ones, for the good ones have been killed."

Nevertheless, this was one order which was not carried out, largely because the speed of the Allied and Russian advance prevented it, but also because Speer and others traveled desperately all over Germany countermanding the mad order.

On April 25, American and Russian forces met at the town of Torgau on the Elbe River. Germany was cut in half—and Hitler was trapped in Berlin. The *Goetterdaemmerung* (Twilight of the Gods), the mythical death of the pagan German gods as celebrated in the turgid operas of Richard Wagner, Hitler's favorite composer, was about to begin.

Now living wholly underground in the large and well-equipped bunker beneath the Chancellery ruins in Berlin, Hitler turned to astrology for comfort. He and Goebbels pored over his horoscope and discovered that within the very near future a decisive change in their fortunes could be expected. Things might look black now, but the stars promised relief. And when, on

April 12, news came of the death of President Franklin D. Roosevelt, Goebbels and Hitler were certain that the turning point had come. Champagne was drunk and hysterical congratulations exchanged.

Hitler was now joined in his underground bunker by the entire Goebbels family—and by Eva Braun, who arrived on April 15. Eva Braun had long been Hitler's unacknowledged mistress and seems to have been genuinely in love with him. In any event she elected to share his death with him. Her very existence was unsuspected by all but a few in Germany. She had remained a virtual prisoner in Hitler's villa at Berchtesgaden, passing her time restlessly between visits of the busy Nazi dictator. She has been described as attractive but possessed of almost no mentality.

Hitler celebrated his last birthday, on April 20, 1945, in the company of his oldest associates. To the small party in the bunker came Hermann Goering, Heinrich Himmler, Joachim von Ribbentrop, Martin Bormann (who replaced Rudolf Hess as the Fuehrer's "Deputy"), Admiral Doenitz, Field Marshal Keitel— and others. They all drank to Hitler's health. And then they ran. That very night Himmler, Goering, and Ribbentrop escaped from Berlin, determined to get away before the Russians closed the last remaining escape routes. Goering, typically, made off at the head of a caravan of trucks full of the art works he had stolen from all over Europe. But Hitler had decided to remain. He was still hopeful that the Russians "would suffer the bloodiest defeat of all before Berlin."

Who was to administer this defeat was a problem which no longer bothered Hitler. At his daily military staff conferences (which continued to the very last) he fumed and raged and fretted over "armies" and "forces" and "attacks" and "counterattacks"—which did not in fact exist. When staff officers tried to tell him that his directives were falling into thin air, Hitler simply flew into one of his rages and refused to listen. Until nearly the last moment Der Fuehrer imagined that German divisions were trying to get through the Russian lines to save him and Berlin. But the shattered German forces around the besieged capital were intent now only on trying to make their way west to surrender to the Allies rather than the Russians.

By April 23, Hermann Goering, who had reached temporary safety in Bavaria, was faced with a dilemma. He was the number two man in Germany, and on many occasions Hitler had decreed that Goering was to succeed him as dictator. Now, with Der Fuehrer cut off in Berlin, Goering wondered whether the moment to assume command had not arrived. He composed a careful telegram to Hitler in which he asked whether, in view of the circumstances, he should assume power as head of state.

Hitler's reaction to this message was to send a telegram in answer in which he informed Goering that he had committed high treason, for which the penalty would be death, but that because of his long service his life might yet be spared if he resigned all his offices immediately. Meantime orders went out from the bunker and by dawn on April 25, Hermann Goering found himself a prisoner of the SS.

To friends in the bunker Hitler shrieked: "Now nothing remains. Nothing is spared me. No allegiances are kept, no honor lived up to, no disappointment that I have not had, no betrayals that I have not experienced, and now this above all else! Nothing remains. Every wrong has already been done me!"

Three days later (on April 26) the first Russian shells began landing on the Chancellery grounds above the bunker. Life within had become hopelessly lunatic. Hitler spent his time planning military campaigns for the relief of Berlin with forces that did not exist. Some among his followers—including Josef Goebbels and his wife—made plans for their own suicide when the Russians should arrive. Martin Bormann and certain of the staff officers seem to have spent much energy plotting how they would escape before the end and how they might ally themselves with whoever inherited Hitler's power in Germany. The fact that only the Allies and the Russians could possibly inherit that power seems to have escaped them.

It also escaped Heinrich Himmler. For some time now he had been in secret negotiations, behind Hitler's back, with the British through agents in Stockholm. He hoped that if he surrendered to the Allies, he might retain some measure of power in an alliance directed against the Russians! That this was a mad hope does not seem to have penetrated Himmler's maniacal mind.

The news that Himmler had contacted the British regarding a surrender reached the underground bunker in Berlin on the evening of April 28. Hitler fell into a spasm of rage such as he had never displayed before. His face turned purple and became unrecognizable as he ranted and roared and finally collapsed onto a chair. This was the worst treachery of all, he screamed to those around him. Although he issued orders for Himmler's arrest, he could not now be sure of vengeance on the SS chief personally. So he ordered one of Himmler's aides unfortunate enough to be present to be taken up to the Chancellery grounds and shot.

A few hours later, news was received that the Russians were now only one block away from the bunker. Their progress through burning Berlin had been resisted desperately by fanatical SS troops and forlorn battalions of young boys—all of whom were being sacrificed to prolong Der Fuehrer's life for a few more hours. It was estimated that the Russians would storm the bunker on April 30.

This was the end, and even Hitler realized it. In the early hours of April 29, Hitler married Eva Braun. He had always resisted her pleas of marriage on the ground that it would interfere with his leadership of Germany. But now, in the last hours of her life, he decided to reward her loyalty by marrying her. Later there was a wedding party—a macabre affair from which Hitler departed to dictate his last will and testament in the next room.

Hitler's will and testament, which came to light after the war, were nothing more than one long repetition of all the lies, distortions, and mad dreams he had hurled at the world for years. The First World War had been "forced" on Germany, the Second World War had been provoked by "Jewish statesmen," he himself had "always wanted" peace. Germans were "not giving up the struggle," because although it was defeated for the moment, there would one day be a glorious "rebirth of the National Socialist movement." He specifically expelled both Goering and Himmler from the Nazi party and designated Admiral Doenitz as his successor.

At noon that same day, April 29, Hitler dictated his last message. In it he once again blasted the German generals and the General Staff (which he had already almost completely wiped out) as betrayers and cowards. He also advised that "The efforts and sacrifices of the German people in this war have been so great that I cannot believe they have been in vain. The aim must still be to win territory in the east for the German people." Those very words might have been spoken by every German leader since the days of Frederick the Great and before. That ancient dream of conquest of the Slavic east was Hitler's last word to his people.

It was during the afternoon of April 29 that news of Mussolini's death was brought to Hitler. The Italian dictator and his mistress, Clara Petacci, had been caught by Italian partisans on April 26 while trying to escape into Switzerland. They had been shot and their bodies thrown into the gutters of Milan.

Hitler now commenced preparations for his own death. He had his favorite dog, Blondi, poisoned and two other pet dogs shot. He passed out poison capsules to his female secretaries in case they wished to use them before the Russians broke in. Then he retired to his private quarters after ordering that no one was to go to bed in the bunker until further orders. At about 2 A.M. on April 30, Der Fuehrer once more appeared and said solemn good-bys to all those who remained in the bunker—and returned to his rooms. After he had gone, the tension suddenly snapped. People started to dance, to drink—to have a party. At this most dreadful moment of their lives, Hitler's last remaining followers broke into a half-hysterical sort of joy. The dancing went on until dawn.

On the following day, April 30, Hitler finished his vegetarian lunch at about 2:30 P.M. He and Eva Braun made another round of farewells to their more intimate friends. Then they retired once again to their rooms. Those waiting in the corridor outside heard a pistol shot. After a few moments they entered Der Fuehrer's rooms. Hitler had shot himself through the mouth with a pistol;* Eva Braun had taken poison. Both were dead. The time was 3:30 on Monday, April 30, 1945. Hastily, Hitler and Eva Braun's bodies were carried up to the Chancellery grounds. There, while Russian shells exploded uncomfortably close, gasoline was poured onto them and they were burned. Goebbels watched, making the outstretched Nazi salute as the earthly remains of his leader ascended in acrid smoke.

Goebbels himself had already planned his own end.

---

* The report of a Soviet investigation was made public in 1968 in *The Death of Adolf Hitler* by Lev Bezymenski. According to this account, the Russians recovered the bodies of Hitler and Eva Braun and performed autopsies on them. The Soviet investigators concluded that both Hitler and Eva Braun had died of poisoning and that a valet, carrying out Hitler's order, had then shot Der Fuehrer. The valet, however, has denied this account.

He could not bear to live without his beloved Fuehrer —and neither could his wife. They had also taken it upon themselves to decide that their children—there were six, ranging in age from three to twelve years— would not survive. The next evening, May 1, Goebbels ordered the same physician who had poisoned Hitler's dog to poison his children. The Goebbels children were interrupted in their playing and given the lethal injections that quickly killed them. Then Goebbels and his wife climbed up to the Chancellery grounds and had themselves shot by an SS man. Their bodies too were burned. The next day the Russians arrived.

One week later Admiral Doenitz, who was now the head of whatever remained of the German state, sent his emissaries to Eisenhower's headquarters—a little red schoolhouse at Reims in France. There, at 2:41 on May 7, 1945, the Germans surrendered unconditionally to the Allies and the Russians. After he had affixed his signature to the document, General Alfred Jodl said: "With this signature the German people and the German Armed Forces are, for better or worse, delivered into the hands of the victors. . . . In this hour I can only express the hope that the victor will treat them with generosity." It may have passed through the minds of the assembled Allied generals—especially the French and Russian—to wonder why General Jodl should expect them to treat Germany generously. But nothing was said.

At midnight on May 8, 1945, the guns fell silent throughout Europe. The sudden stillness was almost a shock to the wretched survivors of Hitler's Thousand-Year Reich. After twelve years, four months, and eight days, Nazi Germany had simply ceased to exist. It had vanished like a nightmare with the coming of dawn. The German people and the German land remained— but the German state had disappeared. Starving, clothed in rags, and huddling in the ruins of their cities and towns, completely dependent on the mercy of their conquerors, the citizens of the vanished Third Reich waited for the future in the empty silence of total defeat.

Epilogue

THE WATCH ON THE RHINE

OCTOBER 1, 1946—AND IN THE CROWDED BUT HUSHED courtroom at Nuremberg Fortress, the former leaders of the Third Reich heard their sentences pronounced by the British, French, American, and Russian judges. The trial of Germany's masters had lasted almost one year —a year during which the world's interest had been claimed by new alarms, old fears, baffling problems of a new era. The men who stood uneasily before the bench seemed by now to be antiques, relics of a long-passed age, as they learned their fate.

Hermann Goering, President of the Reichstag, Chief of the Luftwaffe; death by hanging. *Joachim von Ribbentrop,* Nazi Foreign Minister; death by hanging. *Field Marshal Wilhelm Keitel,* Chief of Der Fuehrer's Command Staff; death by hanging. *Dr. Ernst Kaltenbrunner,* Chief of the Gestapo, successor to Reinhard Heydrich; death by hanging. *Alfred Rosenberg,* Party Philosopher, Reich Minister for the Eastern Territories; death by hanging. *Hans Frank,* Governor General of Poland; death by hanging. *Wilhelm Frick,* originator of the anti-Semitic Nuremberg Laws, persecutor of Catholics, Jews, and trade unionists; death by hanging. *Ju-*

lius Streicher, professional Jew-baiter; death by hanging. *Fritz Sauckel*, Chief of the Nazi slave-labor program; death by hanging. *General Alfred Jodl*, Chief of Operations of Hitler's Supreme Command; death by hanging. *Arthur Seyss-Inquart*, betrayer of Austria, Governor of the Netherlands; death by hanging. *Rudolf Hess*, Der Fuehrer's Deputy, Chief of the Nazi party; life imprisonment. *Walther Funk*, Head of the Reichsbank, receiver of articles from extermination camps; life imprisonment. *Admiral Erich Raeder*, Commander in Chief of the German Navy; life imprisonment. *Baldur von Schirach*, Chief of the Hitler Youth; twenty years' imprisonment. *Albert Speer*, Economic Coordinator of the German War Effort; twenty years' imprisonment. *Baron Konstantin von Neurath*, Former German Foreign Minister, "Protector" of Bohemia and Moravia; fifteen years' imprisonment. *Admiral Karl Doenitz*, successor to Raeder as Commander in Chief of the German Navy, successor to Hitler as Head of State; ten years' imprisonment. *Martin Bormann*, Hitler's deputy, sentenced *in absentia;* death by hanging.

Three defendants at Nuremberg were found not guilty. They were Hans Fritzsche, a minor official in Goebbels' Propaganda Ministry; Hjalmar Schacht, the financial wizard who had done so much to aid Hitler's rearmament program but finally wound up in a concentration camp anyhow; and Franz von Papen, the oily diplomat who had served Hitler so well only to find himself also in a concentration camp in the end. But when these three men left the Nuremberg Fortress, they were immediately arrested by German police who had been waiting outside. They were tried for crimes against the German people by a German court and drew stiff prison sentences—though in the end they served very little time.

Those who had been condemned to death mounted the gallows at Nuremberg on October 16, 1946—all except Hermann Goering, who, at the last minute, swallowed poison which had been smuggled into his cell. Thus he followed Hitler, Goebbels, and Heinrich Himmler (who had swallowed poison when apprehended by the British on May 23, 1945) in choosing suicide rather than face the consequences of his unspeakable crimes.

Many of the other men whose activities have been recounted in this book, such as Vidkun Quisling, were returned to the lands in which they had committed their crimes and were there judged and executed. Some, such as Adolf Eichmann, were to escape at first and wait many years before being brought to justice. Others, such as Alfred Krupp von Bohlen und Halbach, head of the mighty Krupp industries, were, in the long run, to escape any punishment at all. The sentences imposed by German denazification courts, on those who escaped judgment at Nuremberg, were to be mild and often delayed for years.

What, in fact, did the surviving German people think of the men who had led them to catastrophe? Immediately after the war it depended very much on who asked the question. If they knew that their interrogator was anti-Hitler, they condemned their Nazi past; if they suspected that the interrogator was indifferent, they did not. Many years of Nazi rule had destroyed their moral fiber, leaving only one overwhelming desire—to survive.

And survive they did. With their homeland divided into British, French, American, and Russian zones of occupation, with Berlin administered jointly by the Allies and the Russians, with all administrative power down to the village level transferred into the hands of their conquerors, with their very existence during the first bitter years after the war dependent on the generosity of the victors, the vanquished German people set out to rebuild their nation. In doing so, some very old and a few new patterns of German behavior became evident.

First of all, there was, of course, the tremendous industriousness and efficiency for which Germans had always been noted. Within two decades after the fall of Berlin this industriousness was to rebuild Germany completely and give her citizens a standard of living such as they had never before enjoyed, one of the highest in the world. Second, there was the old German habit of playing East against West. Although prostrate Germany could not be accused of starting the "Cold War" which was to divide Russia from her former Allies, Germans profited from American fear of the Soviet Union, which contributed to the rebuilding of German industry and the consolidating of the new West German Republic. This was eventually to lead them into a commanding influence in the Western alliance, NATO, to which a reborn German Army was to make a heavy contribution. Third, there was the old German urge to conquer the east—the *Drang nach Osten*. Although German pretensions to regain those eastern territories which had been seized by Poland and Russia after World War II could not be pressed in the face of Soviet power, they were never renounced and, in fact, form an important element in German politics to the present day.

Some aspects of German life seemed gone forever. Thus the General Staff which for so long had played such an important part in German history had not only been abolished—it had been destroyed by war, by Hitler's vengeance, above all by the Polish-Russian seizure of East Prussia and the destruction of the old Junker estates and way of life from which General Staff officers had sprung. Nor did it seem probable that German militarism would ever again set out to conquer the world. In the age of the atom bomb and the continental superpowers such as the United States and Russia, the German potential for war seemed ridiculously small, even to Germans.

Years after the war the West German Republic was to attempt to make some sort of restitution to the Jews for the incredible suffering inflicted upon them by the Third Reich, through reparations payments to the new Jewish state of Israel. Perhaps of greater significance was the fact that a small but intensely dedicated percentage of German youth was to volunteer over the years to go to Israel and work under rugged conditions to help build the new Jewish homeland.

Many questions remain: Has the experience of building a new republic with a much firmer foundation than the old Weimar Republic brought any sort of political maturity to the German people? Have the terrible lessons of defeat finally stilled their martial spirit? Have they learned to accept their historical and geographical position as the people of the middle without dreaming of conquest, east or west? Has the awful experience of mass murder brought a new sense of tolerance into German life? Above all, could it happen again; could the German people find and follow another Hitler?

At the present time that seems almost impossible. But as the English historian, A. J. P. Taylor, observed: "I have almost reached the point of believing that I shall not live to see a third German war; but events have an awkward trick of running in the wrong direction, just when you least expect it."

It is ironic that the Allies seem determined to force upon the German nation that very role of "defender of Western civilization" which has so often in the past brought catastrophe both to Germany and to "Western civilization."

Today British, French, and American troops are still stationed in western Germany. They are no longer there as an occupying army, but rather as allies of the German Federal Republic against any possible aggression from

the east. But while the West maintains this new Watch on the Rhine, it would seem wise to bear in mind that many of the basic problems of German history have not been solved—and until they are, the world will never forget the echo of thousands of jackboots goose-stepping over cobbled streets; of hoarse and hysterical voices shrieking *"Sieg Heil!"*; of the thunder of guns and the screams of the innocent—for such was the legacy left to the conscience of the world and of the German people by the terrible life and murderous death of Nazi Germany.

Bibliography*

AMBRUSTER, HOWARD W. *Treason's Peace*. New York, 1947.

ANDERS, WLADYSLAW. *Hitler's Defeat in Russia*. Chicago, 1953.

ARMSTRONG, HAMILTON F. *Hitler's Reich*. New York, 1933.

BADOGLIO, MARSHAL PIETRO. *Italy in the Second World War*. London, 1948.

BARRACLOUGH, GEOFFREY. *The Origins of Modern Germany*. New York, 1963.

BENEŠ, EDUARD. *Memoirs of Dr. Eduard Beneš*, London, 1954.

BERNADOTTE, FOLKE. *The Curtain Falls*. New York, 1945.

BEZYMENSKI, LEV. *The Death of Adolf Hitler*. New York, 1968.

BORMANN, MARTIN. *The Bormann Letters*. London, 1954.

BRADLEY, GEN. OMAR N. *A Soldier's Story*. New York, 1951.

BRYANT, SIR ARTHUR. *The Turn of the Tide*. New York, 1957.

BULLOCK, ALAN. *Hitler—A Study in Tyranny*. New York, 1952.

* A Suggested Reading List will be found at the end of the Bibliography.

CARR, EDWARD H. *German-Soviet Relations Between the Two World Wars*. Baltimore, 1951.

CHURCHILL, SIR WINSTON. *The Second World War*. 6 vols. New York, 1953.

CIANO, COUNT GALEAZZO. *Ciano's Hidden Diary, 1937-1938*. New York, 1953.

————. *The Ciano Diaries, 1939-1940*, ed. by Hugh Wilson. New York, 1946.

CLAUSEWITZ, KARL VON. *On War*. New York, 1943.

CRAIG, GORDON A. *The Politics of the Prussian Army, 1940-1945*. New York, 1955.

DALLIN, ALEXANDER. *German Rule in Russia, 1941-1944*. New York, 1957.

DAVIES, JOSEPH E. *Mission to Moscow*. New York, 1941.

DEUEL, WALLACE. *People under Hitler*. New York, 1943.

DRAPER, THEODORE. *The Six Weeks' War*. New York, 1944.

DULLES, ALLEN. *Germany's Underground*. New York, 1947.

EISENHOWER, DWIGHT D. *Crusade in Europe*. New York, 1948.

EYCK, E. *Bismarck and the German Empire*. London, 1950.

FEILING, KEITH. *The Life of Neville Chamberlain*. London, 1946.

FITZGIBBON, CONSTANTINE. *20 July*. New York, 1956.

FLEMING, PETER. *Operation Sea Lion*. New York, 1957.

FREIDIN, SEYMOUR, and RICHARDSON, WILLIAM (eds.). *The Fatal Decisions*. New York, 1956.

FULLER, MAJ. GEN. J.F.C. *The Second World War*. New York, 1949.

GALLAND, ADOLF. *The First and the Last*. New York, 1954.

GILBERT, FELIX. *Hitler Directs His War*. New York, 1950.

GILBERT, G. M. *Nuremberg Diary*. New York, 1947.

GISEVIUS, BERND. *To the Bitter End*. Boston, 1947.

GOEBBELS, JOSEF. *The Goebbels Diaries, 1942-1943*, ed. by Louis P. Lochner. New York, 1948.

GOERLITZ, WALTER. *History of the German General Staff*. New York, 1953.

GUDERIAN, GEN. HEINZ. *Panzer Leader*. New York, 1952.

HANFSTAENGL, ERNST. *Unheard Witness*. New York, 1957.

HASSELL, ULRICH VON. *The Von Hassell Diaries, 1938-1944*. New York, 1947.

HEIDEN, KONRAD. *Hitler—A Biography*. New York, 1936.

HITLER, ADOLF. *Mein Kampf*. Boston, 1943.

Hitler's Secret Conversations, 1941-1944. New York, 1953.

JASPER, KARL. *The Question of German Guilt*. New York, 1947.

KESSELRING, ALBERT. *A Soldier's Record*. New York, 1954.

KOGON, EUGEN. *The Theory and Practice of Hell*. New York, 1951.

KUBIZEK, AUGUST. *The Young Hitler I Knew*. Boston, 1955.

LANGER and GLEASON. *The Undeclared War, 1940-1941*. New York, 1953.

LANGSAM, WALTER C. *Historic Documents of World War II*. Princeton, 1958.

LIDDELL HART, B. H. *The German Generals Talk*. New York, 1948.

———— (ed.). *The Rommel Papers*. New York, 1953.

MANSTEIN, FIELD MARSHAL ERIC VON. *Lost Victories*. Chicago, 1958.

MARTIENSEN, ANTHONY K. *Hitler and His Admirals*. New York, 1949.

MUSSOLINI, BENITO. *Memoirs 1942-1943*. London, 1949.

NAMIER, SIR LEWIS B. *In the Nazi Era*. London, 1952.

OLDEN, RUDOLF. *Hitler, the Pawn*. London, 1936.

PAPEN, FRANZ VON. *Memoirs*. New York, 1953.

PERTINAX. *The Grave Diggers of France*. New York, 1944.

PRANGE, GORDON W. (ed.). *Hitler's Words*. Washington, 1944.

RAUSCHNING, HERMANN. *Time of Delirium*. New York, 1946.

REED, DOUGLAS. *The Burning of the Reichstag*. New York, 1934.

REITLINGER, GERALD. *The Final Solution*. New York, 1953.

RIESS, CURT. *Josef Goebbels: The Devil's Advocate*. New York, 1948.

SCHACHT, HJALMAR. *Account Settled*. London, 1949.

SCHLABRENDORFF, FABIAN VON. *They Almost Killed Hitler*. New York, 1947.

SCHMIDT, PAUL. *Hitler's Interpreter*. New York, 1951.

SCHROETER, HEINZ. *Stalingrad*. New York, 1958.

SCHUSCHNIGG, KURT VON. *Austrian Requiem*. New York, 1946.

SHIRER, WILLIAM L. *Berlin Diary*. New York, 1941.

———. *End of a Berlin Diary*. New York, 1947.

———. *The Rise and Fall of the Third Reich*. New York, 1960.

SKORZENY, OTTO. *Skorzeny's Secret Memoirs*. New York, 1950.

SPEIDEL, GEN. HANS. *Invasion 1944*. Chicago, 1950.

TAYLOR, A. J. P. *The Course of German History*. New York, 1946.

TAYLOR, TELFORD. *Sword and Swastika*. New York, 1952.

———. *The March of Conquest*. New York, 1958.

THYSSEN, FRITZ. *I Paid Hitler*. New York, 1941.

TOYNBEE, ARNOLD (ed.). *Hitler's Europe*. London, 1954.

TREVOR-ROPER, H. R. *The Last Days of Hitler*. New York, 1947.

Trials of War Criminals before the Nuremberg Tribunals. 15 vols. GPO. Washington, D.C. 1952.

WEIZSAECKER, ERNST VON. *The Memoirs of Ernst von Weizsaecker*. London, 1951.

WERTH, ALEXANDER. *Russia at War*. New York, 1964.

WHEATLEY, RONALD. *Operation Sea Lion*. London, 1958.

WHEELER-BENNETT, JOHN W. *Wooden Titan: Hindenburg.* New York, 1936.

————. *The Nemesis of Power.* New York, 1953.

YOUNG, DESMOND. *Rommel—The Desert Fox.* New York, 1950.

ZIEMER, GREGOR. *Education for Death.* New York, 1941.

Suggested Reading:

BULLOCK, ALAN. *Hitler—A Study in Tyranny.* New York, 1952. (An excellent study of Hitler's progressive megalomania.)

DULLES, ALLEN. *Germany's Underground.* New York, 1947. (An account of the plots to kill Hitler.)

GILBERT, G. M. *Nuremberg Diary.* New York, 1947. (A study of the rulers of the Third Reich face to face with justice.)

GOERLITZ, WALTER. *History of the German General Staff.* New York, 1953. (A fascinating study of the General Staff, abridged from the German.)

HEIDEN, KONRAD. *Hitler—A Biography.* New York, 1936. (Especially valuable for Hitler's early years.)

SHIRER, WILLIAM L. *The Rise and Fall of the Third Reich.* New York, 1960. (By far the best popular history of Nazi Germany yet published.)

TREVOR-ROPER, H. R. *The Last Days of Hitler.* New York, 1947. (Exciting account of Germany's death agony.)

Index